I0815278

THE CHILDREN OF CHARLES THE SECOND

By the same author

History and historical biography

Alfred: Queen Victoria's Second Son (2011)
The Prussian Princesses: The Sisters of Kaiser Wilhelm II (2014)
Queen Victoria and the European Empires (2016)
The End of the German Monarchy (2017)
The End of the Habsburgs (2019)

Edited by

Ena and Bee: Queen Victoria's Spanish Granddaughters, Ana de Sagrera (2022)

Music

Jeff Lynne: The Electric Light Orchestra, Before and After (2015)
Pop Pickers and Music Vendors: David Jacobs, Alan Freeman, John Peel, Tommy Vance, Roger Scott (2016)
A Beatles Miscellany (2016)
We Can Swing Together: The Story of Lindisfarne (2017)
Electric Light Orchestra: Song by Song (2017)
While You See a Chance: The Steve Winwood Story (2018)
Led Zeppelin: Song by Song (2018)
All Around My Hat: The Steeleye Span Story (2019)
Kate Bush: Song by Song (2021)

THE CHILDREN OF CHARLES THE SECOND

THE MERRY MONARCH'S FOURTEEN BASTARDS

JOHN VAN DER KISTE

FONTHILL

First published in Great Britain in 2025 by
Fonthill
An imprint of
Pen & Sword Books Ltd
Yorkshire – Philadelphia
www.fonthill.media

ISBN 978-1-78155-946-8

A CIP catalogue record for this book is available from the British Library.

Typeset in Sabon LT 10/13
Typeset by Fonthill
Printed and bound in the UK by CPI Group (UK) Ltd, Croydon, CR0 4YY

The Publisher's authorised representative in the EU for product safety is Authorised Rep Compliance Ltd., Ground Floor, 71 Lower Baggot Street, Dublin D02 P593, Ireland.
www.arccompliance.com

For a complete list of Pen & Sword titles please contact
PEN & SWORD BOOKS LIMITED
47 Church Street, Barnsley, South Yorkshire, S70 2AS, England
E-mail: enquiries@pen-and-sword.co.uk
Website: www.pen-and-sword.co.uk

Or
PEN AND SWORD BOOKS
1950 Lawrence Rd, Havertown, PA 19083, USA
E-mail: Uspen-and-sword@casematepublishers.com
Website: www.penandswordbooks.com

CONTENTS

INTRODUCTION

To research and write about the lives of King Charles II's bastards is an absorbing, fascinating, yet anything but straightforward task, almost a case of 'fools rush in where angels fear to tread'. Much has been written about his mistresses, and in the absence of indisputable information, some of these accounts over the last 300 years freely contradict each other. Any biographer has to accept that fact and fiction about many individuals from the seventeenth century are sometimes inextricably combined, their life stories poorly documented with dubious authentication for statements from contemporary chroniclers and half-truths that rely on a degree of hearsay and imagination in order to try and flesh out a very sketchy existing narrative. For Hanoverian kings, queens, and their families, there is often a fairly solid paper trail of private correspondence to help bring the characters to life, inevitably lacking in the case of the Stuarts and earlier dynasties. To borrow the words of Elizabeth, countess of Longford, when pondering the veracity or lack of it about various details concerning the early life and loves of Queen Victoria's father Edward, duke of Kent, 'so luxuriantly grows the ivy on the bare wall'.[1]

Details about the mistresses of kings and the children that resulted from their liaisons, in this case 'the expensive brood whom Charles's amorous profligacy entailed on his subjects' in the words of Victorian historian John Heneage Jesse, have not always been considered a suitable subject for polite conversation.[2] Queen Victoria and one of her granddaughters,

Victoria, marchioness of Milford Haven (and probably many others of the family), were bored by any idle talk of love affairs and had no time for gossip. 'Either you were married, or not married, and anything in between was a bore.'[3] His reign of almost twenty-five years was something of a golden age for the country in that the arts and sciences were allowed to flourish anew, after the drab philistinism of the Commonwealth interlude.

Yet the Merry Monarch went down in history as one of the most dissolute of our monarchs, and his reputation plummeted during the Victorian age, the general view being that he had the morals of an alley cat. Even some of his contemporaries looked askance at his court's lack of morals and gross extravagance. He had been on the throne for little more than a year when the diarist Samuel Pepys reported on the comments of a friend who complained to him bitterly on 'the lewdness and beggary of the court, which I am feared will bring all to ruin again'.[4]

In a remote age like that of the Stuarts, when it was easier for royalty to keep their personal lives as private as they wished to, the documentation—in the form of correspondence, diaries, and memoranda—is not there. There were always diarists and gossips ready to record or pass on information that was sometimes distorted, but this still sometimes leaves something of a blank or at least not too well-filled canvas. As the ever-helpful and authoritative work *Royal Bastards* by Peter Beauclerk-Dewar and Roger Powell has reminded us, even in the last two centuries, speculation has sometimes arisen along the lines of 'wasn't so-and-so a royal by-blow?' and some parentages have not been officially acknowledged. Even King Charles II and his mistresses themselves, in an era where fidelity to one partner was rare, were sometimes uncertain as to whether he was the father of a certain child, or another lover from aristocratic or court circles with whom the mother had slept. Nobody in the Stuart era had access to DNA or paternity testing for a positive answer. *Cokayne's Complete Peerage*, the magisterial work of reference first published in the late nineteenth century, states that there were fourteen altogether, as far as we know. It might be a couple more, a couple less, but let us accept that as the most likely figure.

In presenting this navigation through a sometimes-obscured path across and between the tangled lines of royal genealogy and sometimes disputed descent from the Merry Monarch, I hope to have presented a reasonably accurate portrayal of who was who, as well as some assessment of their place in royal history.

Particular thanks are due to my publisher, Alan Sutton, who recommended the absorbing subject as a book in the first place; to Sue Woolmans, for the supply of useful research materials; to my editors, Josh Greenland and Jamie Hardwick; and to my wife, Kim, as ever for her support during the several months spent in writing.

I

PRINCE CHARLES

1.

On 13 May 1629, four years after their wedding, Queen Henrietta Maria presented her husband, King Charles I, with a son and heir. The first three years of their marriage had been overshadowed by his unashamed preference for the company of George Villiers, duke of Buckingham. A senior courtier and statesman, he had been a favourite of the previous king, James I, until his death in 1625. It was a privileged position he maintained during the first three years of Charles's reign, much to the annoyance of Henrietta Maria. The situation would persist unhappily until the duke, one of the most thoroughly unpopular men of his time, was stabbed to death by a disgruntled army officer who was far from alone among his countrymen in harbouring a grudge against him. King Charles was at first inconsolable after his devoted companion's violent death, but out of evil came forth good. It had the effect of changing relations between husband and wife much for the better, and they remained close until his own death on the scaffold twenty years later.

Nine months later, in May 1629, Henrietta Maria gave birth to their first child. Sadly, Prince Charles James was a sickly baby who died within a few hours.

Exactly one year later, a second son was born; he was also named Charles after his father. In due course, he would have two younger brothers and five sisters, although one of the latter died on the day of her birth and another only lived to the age of three. Charles was a healthy infant, with an unusually dark complexion, ascribed to the Italian blood on his mother's side. It would later be rumoured by his enemies, although without foundation, that he had been fathered by a 'black Scotsman', and was sometimes pejoratively known as that 'black bastard'.[1] Unlike his father, who was little more than 5 feet tall, as an adult Charles grew to over 6 feet.

In another aspect, as an adult he would prove to be the exact opposite of his father. Charles I always remained faithful to his wife, and no rumours of his having children being born the wrong side of the blanket would ever surface. His namesake son would have no less than fourteen, and according to some sources, possibly seventeen, if not even more. This was not unusual for the time, as his contemporary and brother-in-law, King Louis XIV of France, had twelve illegitimate children as well as six legitimate ones by his wife. His second son, James, who would also become king, had twenty children (five stillborn) by two wives, and another six, possibly seven, by two mistresses. According to the French courtier Philibert, count de Grammont, a keen observer of English court life and its foremost personalities, James had appeased his conscience by marrying, and he thus 'thought that he was entitled by this generous effort to give way a little to his inconstancy'.[2] Monarchs of the later seventeenth century on both sides of the Channel were uncommonly famous (if not infamous) for their inconstancy. Louis had the temerity to scoff at his cousin of England, said John Evelyn to his fellow diarist Samuel Pepys: 'the King of France hath his mistresses, but laughs at the foolery of our King, that makes his bastards princes, and loses his revenue upon them'.[3]

Of Charles II's successors as king, three of the next five would have children out of wedlock while they were married, or four of the next six if a son of the prince regent, later George IV, born after he was living apart from his wife, Caroline, is included. Moreover, King Charles II was not the most prolific in the English regal bastardy stakes. Records suggest that King Henry I, who reigned from 1100 to 1135, had reportedly around twenty-five, in addition to two (maybe three) legitimate children. Ironically, the pregnancies of Queen Catherine, Charles II's consort, resulted in miscarriage or stillbirth. One might consider his large brood as a case of extenuating circumstances if his wife was unable to produce a healthy child.

At his birth, Charles automatically became duke of Cornwall and earl of Rothesay. Although never formally invested, he was designated prince of Wales at around the age of eight. His adolescent years, and those of his siblings, were overshadowed by the approaching storm of a sharply deteriorating relationship between their father and parliament, which he angrily dissolved amid scenes of high drama in 1629 and did not summon again until 1640. The matter culminated in stalemate between the sovereign and his parliamentarians, leading to the outbreak of civil war in 1642. Charles and his brother, James, duke of York, were both present at the first pitched (and inconclusive) battle of Edgehill that year, although being still only boys they were well protected from the line of fire. For a couple of years, they stayed in the royalist capital of Oxford.

In 1645, Charles was sent by his father to the garrison at Bridgwater under the command of Colonel Edmund Wyndham to unite the royalist forces and to hold council. His wife, Christabella, had been Charles's wet-nurse while he was very small. What happened next may or may not have been exaggerated in the interests of a good story. Christabella was said to be 'a celebrated beauty', and more than delighted to meet once again the handsome adolescent prince whom she had probably not seen since he was still a babe in arms.

Edward Hyde, who had been appointed as the prince's governor and father figure to try and make sure he behaved himself in a becoming fashion, was horrified at the spectacle of them both showing undue familiarity with each other in public. She was a married woman, and her husband held a responsible local position in the community. For her and the prince of Wales to be seen kissing and fondling each other in full view of third parties was nothing short of scandalous. Charles was a young man of almost fifteen, in an age when princes were regularly married off in adolescence, and by the standards of the day he was more or less an adult. It has often been said that in times of war, moral standards between a man and a woman thrown together tend to slip, and a sense of 'live for the moment' prevails. While it might be exaggerating to suggest that Mrs Wyndham became the first in a long line of mistresses, the fact remains that she was quite likely his introduction to a life of regular pleasures. As Hyde would later write discreetly in his account of the liaison:

> Being a woman of great rudeness and a country pride, *nihil muliebre praeter corpus gerens* (wearing nothing but a woman's body) she valued

> herself much upon the power and familiarity which her neighbours might see she had with the Prince of Wales, and therefore upon all occasions in company, and when the concourse of the people was greatest, would use great boldness towards him.[4]

There was no opportunity for any moments of passion, or rather lust, to amount to anything of significance. Following successive defeats for King Charles, the west country gradually changed its allegiance towards the parliamentarian army, and the prince's position became untenable. To avoid capture he went into exile, initially to Jersey and then to France, where Queen Henrietta Maria was living at court under the protection of his first cousin, the eight-year-old King Louis XIV, and his regency council. By the summer of 1646, the increasingly beleaguered king had admitted defeat and surrendered.

His French relations seemed reluctant or unable to offer any substantial help to their unfortunate cousins across the Channel. In Holland, Prince Charles's brother-in-law, William II, prince of Orange, and his wife, Charles's sister, Mary, were thought more likely to give some aid to the waning English cause. During the Second Civil War in 1648, which only lasted a few weeks and ended in total defeat for the royalists, Charles moved to The Hague, and it was in this area that he would spend much of his time during the next twelve years.

*****

Charles's enforced idleness in Holland was made bearable by an affair with the woman who had been born Lucy Walter, the name by which she is perhaps best remembered by posterity. In late adolescence, she took the name Mrs Lucy Barlow, and will henceforth be referred to as such. She would be the first of his several mistresses, or rather the first of the well-documented ones, and give birth to the boy destined to be the best-known and ultimately the most ill-fated of his illegitimate children.

After taking into account the somewhat contradictory sources available, it is generally accepted that she was a member of the Welsh gentry, born at the family home, Roch Castle in Pembrokeshire, probably in 1630, which would have made her about the same age as the prince. Her father, William, was a relatively well-off landowner in the area, while her mother, Elizabeth, was a niece of the earl of Carbery, and on marriage had brought with her an ample dowry. Within a few years they had three children, Lucy, John, and Justus. Apparently, William was notoriously unfaithful to his wife, and when she refused to accept the illegitimate children he fathered on their maid as part of the family, he argued and then physically attacked her. Before long she had had enough, and when Lucy was about ten, they separated. She was initially granted financial support against her husband's estates, and took the three children to live with her in London. In 1647, the judgment against William was legally reversed when he brought the same charges of adultery and desertion that she had taken out against him, and she was ordered by the court to return to him with their children.

The only alternative for them was to leave England, and they chose to go and make a new home in the Netherlands, where one of Elizabeth's sisters was already living. They travelled under different names in order to avoid detection and forcible return to the family home, and Lucy Walter became Mrs Lucy Barlow, the latter taken from one of her kinsmen. At this time the title of 'Mrs' did not indicate marriage, but was accorded to non-aristocratic women, with 'Miss' referring to a woman who was someone's mistress rather than wife. During the years that she had spent in London, Lucy had received little if any formal education. All the same, the girl whose childhood had been spent in semi-rural Wales had moved in polite Stuart society enough to act like a young lady of good breeding. She was also very attractive, if not beautiful, by the standards of the day, and would surely never be short of male admirers keen to make her close acquaintance.

Before long, she caught the eye of Algernon Sidney, a staunch republican and parliamentary army officer, son of Robert Sidney, earl of Leicester. The Leicesters were one of many English families 'by the sword divided', as Algernon's younger brother, another Robert, was a groom of the bedchamber to Prince Charles and an army officer. Algernon was said to have come to an informal arrangement with her by which he would pay her fifty pieces of gold for the pleasure of her intimate company. This story, one of many that may or may not be true, probably gave rise more than anything else to the assertion that she was a whore. However, it seems the transaction never went further (unless he made payment and demanded a refund), as he was recalled to his regiment first and she therefore attached herself to his brother, Robert. The fact that he bore arms for the opposite faction evidently counted for nothing in her estimation.

Lucy and Robert therefore travelled to the Netherlands, notwithstanding the disapproval of her mother's family who were already there. Lucy's attractive manner and face did not pass unnoticed among the other royalist officers who had been starved of female company, and Robert evidently realised he could not hope to compete with them for her attention. Fidelity to one partner was presumably not part of her character, and despite her mother's sufferings at the hands of a husband with a wandering eye, she took after her father instead of her mother. A young officer may have been handsome enough, but he was only one of many. When she caught the eye of Prince Charles of the House of Stuart, presumably sometime around the summer of 1648, Robert Sidney realised that he could only come a very poor second.

Some sources suggest she was his first serious love and that they became enamoured of each other when they were still minors, while others indicate perhaps a little implausibly that the prince had had lovers since he was about fourteen. In 1646, he stayed for a while on Jersey, and apparently had a flirtation there, but there is no reliable record of it having led to an affair, let alone the subsequent birth of a child. Claims have been made by contemporaries and discussed by historians ever since that he had a tryst with Marguerite or Margaret de Carteret, wife of Jean de la Cloche, and that the same year she bore Charles a son, who was named Jacques and took her husband's name (and more likely father) as his own. Letters were said to exist as proof, but have been dismissed as forgeries.

Stateless and without any definite prospects for the future, and with his once-mighty father now a prisoner at Carisbrooke Castle on the Isle of Wight, Charles had nothing else to do but hope that the fluctuating prospects of his family might improve—and at the time he had little reason to be optimistic. Had it not been for the war in England, he could probably have had his choice of almost any suitable princess in Europe. There were indeed suggestions of a match between him and his cousin, Sophia, daughter of Frederick V, Elector Palatine, and his wife Elizabeth, daughter of James I, 'the Winter King and Queen of Bohemia', when he was lodged in the palace with them in 1648. It was noticed that he seemed to enjoy her company more than that of her two elder sisters, but the idea came to nothing. A few nights of passion with Mrs Barlow were his only diversion until the call came for him to join a royalist fleet that was planning to sail for England. Yet fortune still favoured the Parliamentarians, and their ships were forced to turn back to the Netherlands before reaching the English coast. By September 1648, he was once again no more than a helpless observer from afar of the king's last ignominious months. He was also now about to become a father himself.

*****

Most historians believe there was never any form of marriage between Charles and Lucy, and never even any suggestion of a binding agreement. Nobody can say for certain that they never secretly went through some ceremony, especially when one considers that his brother, James II, did the same thing with his first wife, Anne Hyde, daughter of the man who would become Charles's lord chancellor—admittedly as a mature man in his late twenties and not as an adolescent, and rather more in the public eye. Rumour has it that Lucy was 'legally married' to Charles on the continent, either in Liège or in Paris; or that Charles may have misled Lucy into believing somehow that they were thus united in an effort to persuade her to have a relationship with him.

Yet a carefree girl of about eighteen who had probably already lost her virginity elsewhere probably needed no persuasion to let herself be bedded by the man who was first in line to the British throne, even a wavering one with an uncertain future. Although many a mistress of a king of England in earlier times had made the most of her time before being callously discarded in favour of 'the next in line', she could have been forgiven for imagining, no matter how implausibly, that a destiny as Queen Lucy might be within her reach.

The only fact beyond dispute is that by September 1648 she was carrying his child. Her pregnancy coincided with the nadir of the British crown's fortunes. In January 1649, King Charles I was tried on a charge of having 'traitorously and maliciously levied war against the present Parliament and the people therein represented', found guilty, and beheaded in front of shocked, if not disbelieving crowds.[5] The Commonwealth proclaimed a British republic, although staunch monarchists never wavered from their view that from 30 January onwards his eldest son was their lawful sovereign King Charles II. He was declared king of Great Britain, France, and Ireland in February by the Covenanter Parliament of Scotland at Edinburgh. As a nation, the Scots were monarchist and ill-disposed to accept an act of abolition forced on them by the English. He was refused permission to enter Scotland unless he solemnly agreed to establish

Presbyterianism as the state religion in all three kingdoms under his rule. That same month, he was also declared king, in French—on Jersey, where a new seal was designed for him.

Charles may have talked to Lucy of marrying her, but if he did, such considerations were not a high priority for him. On 9 April 1649, she gave birth to a son at her uncle's house at Rotterdam. He was named James, and Charles acknowledged him as his own child. Even though Lucy was said to be more than a little free with her favours, this should have been sufficient to dispel any lingering doubts about his paternity. Charles did not acknowledge or admit to having fathered every child who was said at one time to be his offspring, but he never doubted his paternity of James, who bore a striking physical resemblance to him. He had assumed responsibility for the child from his birth, and had his doubts about the suitability of Lucy as a responsible mother.

Yet there could be no question of them living together as husband and wife. Nobody could be so bold as to hazard a guess on whether the English republic would last for years or merely prove to be a doomed experiment. How much Charles saw of baby James during the latter's first few weeks of life is unknown, but before long he was on the move to Paris to visit his own mother, then established at the centre of a court in exile at Saint-Germain-en-Laye, one of the main residences of the French monarchy in the suburbs of Paris. The baby was sent away to a wet-nurse who was placed under the care of an English nurse at the house of Mr Claes Ghysen in Rotterdam, while Lucy went to live in Antwerp, probably in a house belonging to Mrs Hervery.

In August, she went to France and joined Charles. While on her travels, she briefly shared a coach with the writer and diarist John Evelyn. Later he left a brief account of taking a carriage to go and kiss his majesty's hand, referring to her as 'a brown, beautiful, bold but insipid creature'.[6] Her relationship with Charles appears to have carried on in fits and starts for another few months, and she was with him in Paris and perhaps Jersey as well. In June 1649, Charles returned from The Hague to Paris for about three months, and she accompanied him there. Later he returned to the Netherlands, and after that to Scotland. In January 1651, on New Year's Day, he was crowned at Scone Palace, near Perth. At the ceremony, he took an oath, including a commitment to uphold the National Covenant and Solemn League and Covenant, by which he agreed he would impose Presbyterianism on England for three years.

Although Lucy's movements were not well-documented, it was probable that her liaison with Charles continued for at least a year or two after the birth of their child. He was quite short on funds, but somehow he provided enough to let her live in reasonable comfort. Matters were made easier for her especially as she apparently had little or no responsibility for looking after her son. Earnings from 'the oldest profession' may also have supplemented her income. She presumably knew better than to expect a gentle domestic life with a partner whom she might have hoped to look upon as a husband in such unsettled times; if not, she would be rapidly disillusioned. Charles was always known for having a wandering eye, while Lucy's past had hardly been spotless, and nor presumably was her present.

Having travelled around a good deal in her twenty years or so of life, she must have been a woman of the world who appreciated that as long as she did not bite the hand that fed her too hard, she could surely look forward to a regular allowance for herself and her son, plus a certain amount of respect if she behaved herself with dignity. The father of her child was certainly not living in regal luxury, although he was able to live and travel as he needed, perhaps thanks to the bounty of those who were on his side. He seems to have made some financial provision for her and their son, even if his funds never amounted to a regular allowance.

What she may not have appreciated was that Charles wanted custody of his son. James was about a year old when his father sent John Eliot, one of his grooms of the bedchamber, to remove him from his mother's care, with force if necessary. One day, probably in the summer of 1650, she was invited to the Rotterdam fair, leaving the little boy at home with his nurse, and when she returned, she found him gone. Whether the nurse had been part of a plan hatched behind Lucy's back, or a blameless, helpless, and horrified bystander unable to do anything, is not known. Acting on presumably false information deliberately supplied to her to throw her off the scent, Lucy summoned a horse-drawn carriage and went to the port of Maassluis, from where she had been told he was to be taken to England. Although she made a scene and attracted a large crowd, nothing came of it. A few days later, he was discovered in a house in a village close to The Hague, being looked after by a couple of Eliot's accomplices. He was promptly returned to his mother.

She took him to Paris for his safety, where she had a casual fling with a Colonel Bennet, and a rather more lasting one with the royalist officer

Theobald, Viscount Taaffe, later earl of Carlingford. About thirty years older than her, he had been married and was probably a widower. In May 1651, she gave birth to a daughter, Mary, and either Taaffe or Bennet (the former being thought more likely) was almost certainly the father. Lucy and Taaffe were living together at the Louvre, much to Henrietta Maria's indignation, but she could not persuade them to find somewhere else and leave. Taaffe was keeping her and her children, and the queen regent and Cardinal Mazarin were both so preoccupied by the Fronde Revolution that they ignored her complaints about the infamous Mrs Barlow's troublemaking and rudeness.

Charles and Lucy's liaison had run its course, but he allowed her and Taaffe to remain under the same roof as himself, as long as he did not have to pay for her and could maintain contact with his son. He liked Taaffe, whose morals were not beyond reproach—as was the case with the ever-libidinous prince himself—and his skills as a military commander were slight, but he was good company and assured there was never a dull moment if he was around.

Meanwhile, Prince Charles (or King Charles II, as his most faithful supporters regarded him) was preoccupied with more weighty matters. The parliamentarians had shown themselves good at winning battles and may have executed their last monarch, but Oliver Cromwell's position as lord protector, presiding over the Commonwealth of England, Scotland, and Ireland, was still in its infancy and not regarded as secure. The Scots had some residual loyalty to the crown, the Stuarts having been a dynasty north of the border since the fourteenth century. North of Hadrian's Wall lay Charles's best hope of restoration, and on New Year's Day 1651, he was crowned king of Scotland.

Yet his position remained vulnerable to attack from his enemies, and it was decided to take the campaign for his reclaiming the crown to the heart of England. He therefore placed himself at the head of what was mainly a Scottish army, with a few English royalists who were recruited to the ranks as the soldiers proceeded south. It culminated in an invasion that was halted by defeat at the Battle of Worcester on 3 September 1651, for in what would be the last major engagement of the civil wars, he was greatly outnumbered by his adversaries and defeated. He escaped from England and landed in Normandy on 16 October, despite a reward of £1,000 on his head, and almost certain death for anyone who was caught helping him to flee.

Later that month, he returned from Scotland to The Hague and when he went to Paris, Lucy Walter went there too. Others say he cut off all contact with her at this point, but it appears this was not the case and that he continued to correspond with her, as well as promising her an allowance (that may not necessarily have always been paid) and give her an expensive pearl necklace. Even so, whatever passion there may have been on his side had run its course. The rumours about her misconduct and loose living disturbed him, and he had sufficient feelings as a father to try and ensure that the boy was given a proper upbringing, something that she seemed incapable of providing for him. Moreover, it would reflect ill on him if he was seen to be sharing his life with her while receiving much-needed funds from time to time of King Philip IV of Spain, who set great store by personal morality, as did the aptly named Puritan regime in England. A hopeful king-in-waiting who was intent on reclaiming his throne would not find his cause helped by being inextricably linked with a mistress who behaved like a reckless good-time girl.

Lucy was also romantically involved with Sir Henry de Vic, Charles's representative in Brussels at this time, and may have considered him as a potential husband, especially as he seemed comfortably well off. Any insistence that she was legally married to Charles had evidently long since been abandoned. It is said that Lucy and Sir Henry went to Cologne together to obtain permission but this was refused, de Vic was reprimanded for leaving his post without leave and he, Lucy, and little James returned to Brussels empty-handed.

In January 1655, Charles consulted his political advisers, Sir Edward Hyde and James Butler, duke of Ormond. They agreed that Lucy should be provided with a pension, not make any further claims on the prince, and conduct herself with more decorum. She and de Vic had now parted company, and she had sole care of six-year-old James, a matter of some concern to his father. Charles then sent her a written promise of £400 a year in four separate instalments, conditional on her good behaviour. A few months after she received the first sum, Lucy and her children came under the protection at The Hague of Colonel Thomas Howard, whose mistress she now became. He was the brother of the earl of Suffolk and master of the horse to Mary of Orange. His wife, Walburga van der Kerckhoven, was governess to the little Prince William of Orange, Mary's only child and also destined to be a future king of England.

A theory suggests that Mary may have deliberately tried to bring Thomas Howard and Lucy together, hoping that she might transfer her attentions from Prince Charles, and that despite being married, Thomas was prepared to play along with the scheme. He was prepared to set Lucy up in her own establishment at Delft, but before she could move into the house, she and young James returned to England.

By now, Lucy was generally disregarded with disfavour. It seems she decided to leave the Dutch Netherlands for those of Spain presumably in order not to be drummed out of The Hague. In Antwerp, she, James, and her daughter were joined by her brothers. After being involved in one scandal after another, causing much embarrassment to the exiled royal court, her reputation stood low. Her mother died in February 1656, leaving all of her estate to her aunt in the Netherlands.

Determined to contest the will, she and her brother, Justus, planned to go to London together. The problems that might ensue with her being left to her own devices in Cromwellian England at such a delicate time spoke for themselves. Charles had a brief meeting with Lucy on 22 May in Antwerp, just prior to her sailing from Flushing for England. Once again, posterity relies on surmise, but he was perhaps taking advantage of any chance to see his young son again, and to suggest that the boy should stay with him while Lucy and Justus went to seek what they believed to be legally theirs.

On arriving in London in June 1656, Lucy and her brother stayed over a barber's shop near Somerset House with Lord Thomas, her children, and a maid, Ann Hill. She was suspected by the authorities of being a royalist spy at The Hague, was under constant surveillance from John Thurloe, Oliver Cromwell's secretary, and soon realised that Howard could no longer be relied on to protect her all the time. Lucy, her children, and Hill were arrested on the protector's orders and taken to the Tower of London to be questioned by Colonel Sir John Barkstead, the lieutenant of the Tower. One of those who sat in judgment at Charles I's trial as well as being a signatory to his death warrant, Barkstead was renowned as one of the hardline regicides, disinclined to show mercy to any of the royalist family or their associates. When he questioned her, she claimed she was the widow of a Dutch sea captain, saying she had returned to England to claim her mother's legacy. Barkstead may have realised that the latter statement was true, but he knew enough about her—probably as a result of speaking to Ann Hill—to realise that the rest was a lie.

When she was asked about the son he was well aware that she had borne as Prince Charles's mistress, she stated that he had died and the children with her had been fathered by the late Dutchman. Barkstead, Cromwell, and his advisers realised she was obviously not a spy, and there was nothing to gain by keeping her as a prisoner. She would probably inflict far more damage on Charles's reputation if she was sent back to Flanders, which was what happened after interrogation and release.

Back on the European mainland, she and Justus planned to renovate the house at Delft. Before this could happen, she became involved in a dispute with a local wine merchant, was arrested, and sent to prison. Finding no help forthcoming from Thomas Howard, she prevailed on Robert Sidney, with whom she had remained on good terms. She decided to sell her house and most of its contents, and move to another property in the Spanish Netherlands. Trouble came when Howard disputed her right to sell the contents, as most of it belonged to him. Deciding she would not get mad but rather get even, she turned for further assistance to one of her cousins, Charles Bursfield, who had recently arrived from England to come and help her in any way she could—by taking Howard's life. When his challenge to fight a duel was not accepted, Bursfield lay in wait for him in an alley with a dagger, close to where the king was lodging. Falling upon his victim, he attempted to kill him but only succeeded in wounding him in the arm.

At about this time, it was said that her brother, John, was in the pay of Cromwell, reporting on Lucy's dealings with Charles, journeying between England and mainland Europe under the alias of Mr Hall. Charles and Edward Hyde were well aware of her exploits, especially as Charles was using the services of Daniel O'Neill, nicknamed 'Infallible Subtle', to keep a close watch on her. He reported on her affair with Thomas Howard, and people in The Hague were so angry that they demanded her expulsion as soon as possible. He was also credited with saying that Lucy's maid was blackmailing her by threatening to make public her adulterous behaviour, as well as stories of two self-induced abortions, and that she was responsible for suggesting that they should dispose of the woman by inserting a needle through her ear and into her brain while she was asleep (at one stage she was accused of murdering a servant, although the charge was subsequently dropped). He advised Charles not to give Lucy any more money, and that if he was prepared to recognise James as his son, they ought to remove the boy from her care as soon as possible.

From Flanders, Lucy went to Paris to find she had been completely disowned by Charles, but he was still sending her messages promising money and support, while publicly denouncing her in an attempt to dissuade her from publishing papers he was keen to obtain. This referred to the documents that she claimed would prove their marriage, presumably those contained in a notorious and quite likely non-existent black box that was said to contain the relevant certificate. She was neglecting the education of their young son of whom she had custody, and continued to harass Charles by threatening him over the papers and jeopardising his position by behaving scandalously while he was dependent upon the goodwill of foreign royalty for his own support. Charles's sister, Mary, and his political advisors regarded Lucy as a menace because her behaviour could damage Charles's prospects with a view to the hoped-for restoration of the monarchy, which was looking increasingly likely as the Commonwealth faltered and Oliver Cromwell and his son, Richard, were rapidly losing popularity in England.

Charles arranged for James and Lucy to be lodged in the house of his agent and Lord Bristol's secretary, Sir Arthur Slingsby, who was meant to keep an eye on her and try to dissuade her from any further misconduct. However, she had just sold the letters Howard had written to her, revealing his activities as a royalist conspirator. She now announced that she was going to 'post up' Charles's letters and their marriage certificate, in full public view, in the Grande Place in Brussels unless he awarded her a much larger pension. This threat prompted Charles to arrange another attempt to kidnap his son, and he ordered Slingsby to remove the boy from his mother's hands. In December 1657, Slingsby tried to have her seized and arrested for failing to pay for her keep, and he attempted to take James from her and have him put in a secure place for his own good. She ran into the street weeping and crying, clutching her son, as passers-by came to her aid. The secretary insisted that he was carrying out his duty on behalf of the English king, but his ill-considered attempt to restrain her immediately brought the crowd on to her side.

It was an embarrassing episode for Charles, and one for which he could hardly deny responsibility. The Spanish ambassador to Charles's exiled court in Brussels, Don Alonso de Cardenas, condemned Slingsby's actions as utterly disgraceful, and immediately offered Lucy and her son his full protection from any further similar action. The failed attempt had serious implications in that it threatened to destroy the amicable relationship between the Spanish royal court and the exiled Stuarts, so carefully nurtured over the previous few years with an eye to the restoration of the latter. Charles was in Bruges when it happened, and the last thing he wanted to do was to lose his hard-earned Spanish support.

At the same time, he could not leave Lucy to her own devices and let her continue to damage his good name by her embarrassing, even lawless actions. In responding to her latest outbursts, he needed to take careful in remaining on the right side of the law and keeping the Spanish on his side. He therefore wrote a carefully worded letter of explanation to Cardenas, stating his case and affirming that he was in fact the wronged party. His primary concern had always been for their child's welfare, as well as for Lucy's well-being herself. Some assistance from Spain to restrain Lucy's actions would be essential in finding a solution. It would, he said, be of great advantage to mother and child, 'if she shall now at length retire to such a way of life that many redeem in some measure the reproach of her past ways'.[7]

The Spanish accepted his version of events and agreed to assist him in his attempts to keep Lucy's provocative behaviour within bounds. She spent Christmas under the watchful eye of Cardenas. Meanwhile, Daniel O'Neill told Slingsby to make sure that the potentially damaging letters that she had so incautiously told the world she had in her possession should be removed from her possession as soon as possible and returned to Charles. Like so much else connected with her and the written evidence of her relationship with Charles, if they had ever existed, they conveniently disappeared.

It was now just a matter of time before she lost her little son. She had presumably been under strict but secret surveillance for a while. One day in April 1658, one of Charles's servants came to call on her, saying he needed to discuss official business. At one point she went to collect some papers, and while her back was turned, he seized the boy and took him out of the house. She immediately began to search for them, but without success.

For months she tried first in Brussels, and then following James to Paris, where he eventually ended up in the care of William Crofts, a royalist politician who was on friendly terms with the king, and whose family name he took for a while. Queen Henrietta Maria assumed responsibility for his upbringing and arranged for him to attend the Oratorian College of Notre Dame des Verlus, near Paris. At one stage his education was supervised by Thomas Ross, a poet and scholar. Ross became fond of his nine-year-old charge, although saddened that he had not been given the chance to acquire the normal basic skills earlier in childhood. To a friend he wrote that it was 'a great pity so pretty a child should be in such hands as hitherto have neglected to teach him to read or tell [count to] twenty though he hath a great deal of wit and a great desire to learn'.[8] It appears that one thing he learnt from, or was rather told by, Ross was that he was the legitimate son of Charles, prince of Wales, and would probably be king one day. If so, it was one piece of misinformation that would have severe repercussions for them all.

Another tutor for a while was Father Stephen Goffe, a former chaplain to King Charles I. He had been arrested for and charged with helping the king to escape from Hampton Court, but after the latter's execution he moved, or was perhaps exiled, to France and remained a friend of Queen Henrietta Maria. His family was a divided one, for his brother had been among the signatories to the king's death warrant.

Lucy probably never saw her son again. Either by her own choice or else under orders, she left Brussels and moved to Paris, apparently suffering from some unspecified illness. Realising that she was not long for this world, she decided to put things in order and at around this time she made a full confession of her sins to John Cosin, who served as chaplain to some members of the household of the exiled royal family and later became bishop of Durham. While she had committed many misdemeanours in her short adult life, she admitted, she remained adamant that she had married King Charles, and allegedly provided Cosin with a certificate which he kept in a black box. This was supposedly passed on after his death to Sir Gilbert Gerard, his son-in-law. She died sometime between the end of August and December 1658, aged about twenty-eight, and was believed to have been buried in the Huguenot cemetery, in the Faubourg Saint-Germain district of Paris.

Charles's eldest brother and heir, James, duke of York, said that Lucy died of a 'disease incident to her profession'.[9] That is possible, even likely, but as her son was an ever-present threat to his status, he had every good reason to besmirch her reputation, and his word cannot be taken at face value. Yet he was not alone in the family in refusing to pay her anything resembling a graceful tribute. Their sister, Mary, princess of Orange, had also regarded her as a major nuisance who by her behaviour had put at risk Charles's likelihood of reclaiming the throne during the Cromwell years. Modern writers are less judgemental and view her as a typical carefree young woman of her age. The verdict of King Charles II's major modern biographer Antonia Fraser is that she was neither a whore nor the chosen bride of the prince of Wales, just one of many girls who belonged 'to that restless and inevitably light-moralled generation of young ladies who grew up in the untrammelled times of the Civil War'.[10] She had found herself in a difficult position, and though her behaviour may not always have been wise or if her conduct as a responsible mother left something to be desired, as she strove to assure herself a comfortable future without financial worries she can hardly be blamed.

*****

Lucy Barlow had been the first of what would be a long line of Prince (later King) Charles's mistresses, some of whom would bear him at least one child. In the lax moral climate of Restoration England and its royal court, there was a free and easy attitude to morality and marital fidelity, or lack of it. Throughout his adult life he had at least one female companion at a time, ready to share his bed. He was also known to pay occasional incognito visits to London brothels, a strange risk for him to take in view of his height and the subsequent difficulty in disguising himself properly, and one can only suppose that he took some strange delight in courting the ever-present danger of discovery. From 1662 onwards, he also had a lawfully wedded wife and consort who came from a European court that was less tolerant of such standards, or lack of them. Ironically, his consort would prove unable to give him a child to secure the succession, a situation that on his death was only solved by disputes that had to be solved by invasion and bloodshed.

The future sovereign's harem, to use a colloquial term, sometimes tolerated each other and even enjoyed friendly, if not particularly close, relations, though they were not above indulging in petty rivalries or hesitating to pour withering scorn on one another. One of the most recent historians to examine the subject in detail, Linda Porter, suggests that Lucy Barlow was the only one he abandoned as she became a liability to his good name. One might use such a term advisedly. She died relatively young, before he was able to reclaim his father's throne. With the others, who all survived him, he retained 'the same kind of easy affection for them', as well as for their joint offspring, as he did for his childless wife.[11]

The second mistress (or at least the second of whom details have been handed down to posterity) was Elizabeth ('Betty') Killigrew. Born in 1622, and thus eight years older than Charles, she came from a well-connected royalist family. One of her brothers, Thomas, served Prince Charles as a diplomat in Italy during the 1650s as well as enjoying a successful career as a dramatist and theatre manager. Another, William, also served at court, becoming Queen Catherine's vice-chamberlain and also a playwright. Their niece, Anne, was a distinguished artist who during her short life painted a portrait of King James II, and whose poetry was published to great acclaim shortly after her death from smallpox at only twenty-five.

Elizabeth was married at nineteen to Francis Boyle, son of the earl of Cork and a well-known Irish royalist officer, later created Viscount Shannon. She joined the royalist court-in-exile in France led by Queen Henrietta Maria as a maid of honour, and it was in this post that she met the young future king. Affairs took their course, and the marriage does not appear to have been damaged by her infidelity. Her husband was rewarded for his compliance by being awarded a viscountcy at the restoration, and subsequently by the governorship of County Cork some twelve years later.

The couple already had two sons and a daughter by the time Elizabeth began her liaison with Charles. Their daughter, Charlotte, was born in Paris in 1650 and took the family name of Fitzroy. Portraits of her, which do not seem to have survived, were said to show a young woman who took after her father in looks.

Charlotte married twice, firstly at the age of thirteen to James Howard, a grandson of the 2nd earl of Suffolk. He was the same age as her and died in 1669. This marriage produced a daughter, named Stuarta, who later became a maid of honour to Queen Mary II and died in 1706. In 1672, Elizabeth took as her second husband William Paston, who later became earl of Yarmouth. They had several children, of whom two sons and two daughters survived childhood.

Elizabeth's date of death is uncertain. Some say she died in her early thirties, perhaps predeceasing her father and sovereign, at the family home in Pall Mall, and was buried in Westminster Abbey, while others suggest she was still alive for another twenty years or so after that. Her widower converted to the Roman Catholic faith, and in 1687, King

James II appointed him treasurer of the household, later also making him lord lieutenant of Wiltshire a year later. Loyal to the Catholic king who lost his throne, he converted to Anglicanism in 1689, but refused to swear allegiance to King William III and Queen Mary after the Glorious Revolution. He was then deprived of his offices, and twice imprisoned in the Tower of London because of his Jacobite sympathies. After being released, he was forgiven and admitted to the House of Lords.

At around this time, Charles also had an affair in Paris with Eleanor Needham, daughter of Viscount Kilmorey and a widow twice over. They had no children, although she managed to obtain some money from him which he had perhaps unwisely promised and then found his straitened circumstances would not permit him to pay. After the Restoration, she obtained a pension of £500 a year from him, rather less than she had hoped for, but perhaps fortunately for him she died about two or three years later.

*****

While he was in Bruges, probably around 1650, Charles had an affair with Catherine Pegge. Born about 1635, she was the daughter of Thomas and Catherine Pegge, royalists in exile who had lived at Yeldersley Old Hall, Derbyshire. During the Civil War, Thomas was captured while serving under the royalist General Henry Hastings, Baron Loughborough, and they went into exile at Bruges. Very little is known about her, or indeed how she and her royal lover came face to face.

Contemporaries spoke of her as one of the great beauties of her age, a distinction so over-used as to become meaningless, and she was thought to have been painted twice by King Charles's principal painter in Ordinary Sir Peter Lely, although the present whereabouts of these pictures are unknown. During Charles's latter years of exile as a prince, she presented him with two children. A son, also named Charles, was born in 1657, and a daughter, Catherine, probably born in 1658 and commonly assumed to have died in early childhood.

This is disputed by a theory that she became a nun at Dunkirk and went by the name Charlotte or Katherine Fitzcharles (Dame Cecilia), dying there in 1759, 'very aged'.[12] As she would thus have lived to a hundred years or more, it sounds unlikely. Both children were thought to have been born in Bruges. Different sources suggest that Catherine Pegge married Sir

Edward Greene of Sampford, Essex, either in July 1660, two months after the restoration, or in 1667. They had a daughter, Justinia, who was born in 1667 and lived to the age of sixty. Sir Edward died at Flanders in 1678 in Flanders, and his body was sent home for burial at Sampford. His widow's name disappeared from history and date of death remains unknown.

Charles, who was initially given the family name Fitzcharles, was brought up by his mother in the Spanish Netherlands with the support of his maternal grandfather, Thomas Pegge of Yeldersley. Very swarthy in appearance like his father, he was commonly known by the nickname 'Don Carlos'.

*****

Generally reckoned to be the most notorious, most grasping, and least liked of King Charles II's mistresses was the one who gave him five, maybe six children: Barbara Palmer. She became countess of Castlemaine on her marriage and was later created duchess of Cleveland in her own right in 1670. She was born in 1640 in the parish of St Margaret's, Westminster, the only child of William Villiers, 2nd Viscount Grandison, and his wife Mary, co-heiress of 1st Viscount Bayning. The viscount had a family connection with the court in that he was a half-nephew of the duke of Buckingham, Charles I's favourite who had been assassinated in 1628. Her first cousin, Elizabeth Villiers, countess of Orkney, would later become a mistress of King William III.

The Villiers family were always pro-royalist, and when the Civil War broke out the viscount readily provided horses and ammunition for the crown at his own expense. He did not live to see the outcome for he was killed while leading a brigade of cavaliers at the storming of Bristol in July 1643 when the royalist army captured the port of Bristol from the parliamentarian garrison. His widow and daughter were left in straitened circumstances, although their ailing fortunes recovered a little when the former married Charles Villiers, 2nd earl of Anglesey, a cousin of her late husband. After the execution of King Charles I in 1649, the impoverished Villiers family secretly transferred its loyalty to his eldest son, although as adherents to the royalist regime they knew they were under constant surveillance. Each year on 29 May, his birthday, young Barbara and the rest of the family went down to the cellar of their home in darkness where they would drink to his health in secret.

By the time of her eighteenth birthday, with her tall, voluptuous figure, masses of brunette hair, and heavy-lidded dark blue eyes, Barbara was considered one of the most beautiful of the royalist women, although one feels such a phrase is probably used somewhat generously. During her life, or one might say her reign, at court, Lely painted nearly all of the king's mistresses at least once, and throughout his career he portrayed Barbara about ten times in all. Lack of family money had left her with somewhat reduced marriage prospects, and she was forced into a marriage of convenience, a financially successful, if personally none-too-happy match when she wedded Roger Palmer, later 1st earl of Castlemaine, on 14 April 1659. A staunch lifelong Roman Catholic, he was the son of a gentleman of the bedchamber under King Charles I. Though her family had been more than pleased to send her to the altar, the union took place against his parents' wishes. They suspected she was not the kind of woman to make any husband a pliant wife, and his father presciently commented that she would make him one of the most miserable men in the world.

Perhaps the elder Mr Palmer already sensed that she had her eye on the greatest catch a woman in England could ever hope for. Events one year later would make that dream come true.

2

CHARLES II

1.

Oliver Cromwell had died from natural causes in September 1658 and his son, Richard, had no desire to try and assume the mantle of his father. Throughout the country, there was no general desire to continue the republican experiment. The Cromwellian dynasty had been and gone; the Stuart dynasty still endured, if more in the breach than the observance. On 25 April 1660, the Convention Parliament, elected as a 'free parliament' with no allegiance to either Commonwealth or to monarchy, assembled at Westminster.

Members unanimously gave a warm reception to the conditions that Charles had promised at the Declaration of Breda. This was a document in which he made several promises if he was called to the throne, among them undertaking to observe lenience and tolerance towards his subjects; granting a 'free and general pardon' for crimes committed during the English Civil War and the Interregnum for all those who recognised him as the lawful king, 'excepting only such persons as shall hereafter be excepted by parliament'; accepting the retention by current owners of property purchased during that time; and to grant any outstanding payment of arrears to members of the army. He would ensure complete liberty of conscience, and a benevolent Anglican church policy; there would be neither exile for past enemies nor confiscation of their wealth; and he would grant pardons for nearly all his opponents except for the regicides.

Finally, he promised that he would rule in cooperation with parliament. These were all the guarantees that parliament required to proclaim him king and invite him back to England.

A convention had been called in Ireland earlier that year and declared for his return as their sovereign, and on 14 May, he was proclaimed king in Dublin. He set out from Holland, arrived in Dover on 25 May 1660, and reached London four days later, on his thirtieth birthday.

Throughout his early years, King Charles II had certainly seen and suffered the slings and arrows of outrageous fortune, and he had taken to heart the defeat of his father in war and his subsequent humiliating execution in public. He knew well what it was like to be a fugitive in his own country and an exile with no certain prospects. Now the wheel had turned full circle, and it was his turn to wear the crown. While he would always be reluctant to trust the English after what had happened, he vowed to reign with a careful commitment to respecting the wishes of people and parliament, knowing how and when to get his own way, bending cautiously to circumstances when he saw it was to his advantage.

As legend has it, he vowed henceforth never to go on his travels again. His brother and successor would lose his throne within four years of succeeding to it, though at least he would escape with his life. Yet when measured against that simple yardstick, the new king kept his crown; their father had signally failed, as would his second son.

Meanwhile, within a few months of the start of Charles's reign, Barbara Villiers would give him a child, the first of several. During the next thirteen years, they became the joint parents of at least four children, and possibly six. This was considerably less than the number of other lovers that she allegedly took during the same period. Her first child, a daughter named Anne, was born on 25 February 1661, and was said to have been conceived in London on the night of the Restoration in England that made Charles Stuart his father's fully recognised successor as king.

Another equally plausible theory has it that Barbara became *enceinte* at The Hague where Charles had gone on 14 May 1660, to prepare for his triumphal return home. She and her husband, Roger, had arrived at the exiled court about three months earlier, and it was at around this time that the affair began. It was not the king-in-waiting's first; but it was not her first either. She had already had a fling with Philip Stanhope, earl of Chesterfield, a notorious ladies' man, who married at least three wives, but there were doubts as to whether he was the father of the second one's daughter. He also had a colourful history behind him, having been imprisoned in the Tower of London after wounding one man in a duel in 1658, killing another in a second duel shortly after his release, and fleeing to Holland early in 1660, then being pardoned by Charles II at the time of the Restoration before returning to England.

King Charles claimed paternity of Barbara's daughter, Anne, as did Chesterfield, and Roger Palmer as well. This unfortunate child of a disputed three-way parentage was said to bear a marked likeness to the two former, particularly Chesterfield who, according to George Legge, who was appointed lieutenant-general of the ordnance in 1660, 'she resembled very much both in face and person'.[1] The cuckolded husband duly received his reward for meekly putting up with this state of affairs, when the king created him Baron Limerick and earl of Castlemaine in 1661. These titles were given on the understanding that they would only be passed down through Roger's heirs by Barbara, and thus providing a way for the king to secure indirectly an inheritance for his illegitimate children.

When she was eight years old, Anne was sent to be educated at Chaillot, France, at the monastery of Queen Henrietta Maria. After the latter's death the following year, she was brought back to England, only for her education to resume at the Abbey of Pontoise, Normandy. She came back to England in November 1672.

On 18 June 1662, Charles Palmer, Barbara's eldest son, was born. She had originally announced that she was going to give birth at Hampton Court. The court had already gathered there to celebrate the king's marriage, for it was thought that for her to do so would be rather tactless, and it was suspected that either her husband or the king had to order her to stay in London instead. As a result, the baby was born at the King Street House that belonged to Roger Palmer. The earl of Castlemaine, a Roman Catholic, had him baptised into the Roman Catholic faith, but six days later the king had him rechristened into the Church of England. When Barbara found out, she was furious. Entering their home at King Street, according to Pepys, 'she left her Lord, carrying away everything in the house; so much as every dish, and cloth, and servant, but the porter. [Roger Palmer] is gone discontented into France, they say, to enter a monastery.'[2]

With this action the marriage, which had never really been anything more than a sham, was over in all but name, and he spent much of the next couple of years in Europe. It was unlikely that he fathered any of his wife's numerous children. Husband and wife officially separated in 1662, after the birth of Charles, who was later given the name Charles Fitzroy. The dire predictions that Roger's father had made about the misery in store for him if he married her had not taken long to be realised.

*****

The separation of the earl and countess of Castlemaine coincided, though not by design, with King Charles's marriage. Negotiations between the English and Portuguese courts for the hand of Catherine of Braganza had begun while Charles I was still on the throne, and allowed to rest in suspended animation until the Restoration. It had been a long interval and, respecting the fact that he could not pass his throne on to a child born out of wedlock, Charles had looked elsewhere for a royal consort who could give him an heir. When some German princesses were suggested, he rejected them at once, dismissing them as 'all dull and foggy'.

On being shown a portrait of Catherine, he was immediately interested in her. What tempted him even more, however, was the prospect of a generous cash dowry, British possession of the port of Tangier on the north African coast, the island of Bombay, and, above all, the prospect of lucrative trading privileges for English seamen in the New World. The marriage contract was signed on 23 June 1661, although England had to wait for several months until her people had a first sight of their queen. She arrived at Portsmouth in May 1662, and a week later the bride and groom were married there in two ceremonies, a Catholic one in secret, followed by an Anglican one.

Catherine, a quiet, even-tempered young woman, had had a very secluded upbringing, and was ill-prepared for leaving her home in a distant country to come and live with a husband who had no meaning of the concept of marital fidelity. She was still at Hampton Court when her introduction to the woman who would be such a thorn in her side took place. Having quickly recovered from giving birth to her first son by King Charles, the countess was living nearby, at her uncle's house in Richmond. In an age during which many women died in childbirth and infant mortality was high, she and her children were exceptionally healthy. It may have been an unfortunate error of judgement, or else tactless in the extreme, of him to introduce his mistress to his wife so suddenly and then proceeding, with a determination bordering on calculated cruelty, to insist that she was one of the ladies of the queen's bedchamber.

One wonders if king and mistress had discussed such a strategy beforehand. Yet whatever he might have declared in his wedding vows, Charles never seems to have had any intention of giving up the countess of Castlemaine, or even adopting a more sensitive course of action that might have enabled his wife and mistress to be kept apart. Instead, Catherine was presented with what a more worldly woman might have shrugged off or accepted as a case of one rule for kings, another for queens. It was hardly a welcoming start to her new life.

Catherine had already been informed as to the presence of her husband's mistress. According to the earl of Clarendon, who had been appointed chancellor of the exchequer just after the restoration and had remained King Charles's foremost adviser, she had decided for herself that she was never going to allow this woman in the same room as her. Those who were closest to her declared that her mother had assured her she would be well within her rights to make such a request, and expect it to be honoured without question. Charles evidently thought otherwise. He thought that he had prepared his bride to give Barbara a civil reception, led her into her chamber and introduced them to each other without expecting any problem.

At first, the appearance of this woman did not appear to Queen Catherine to be of any special significance. She was still struggling with an unfamiliar language of which she could barely speak a word, names, and titles, and either did not hear or more likely did not understand properly the identity or function of this other woman. Nevertheless, she responded graciously and held up her hands to be kissed. There are two versions of what happened next. One says that her chief Portuguese lady in waiting, the countess of Penalva, who was standing behind her chair, whispered in her ear that this was the countess of Castlemaine. Clarendon said later that the queen either recognised her or else guessed her identity at once, as the woman with whom she had intended to have as little to do with as possible. She burst into tears, fainted, and had to be helped to another room.

King Charles seemed oddly unconcerned about his wife's distress, and saw it as an embarrassment, an unwarranted reaction on her part. He may have suspected that that a faction might form around the queen, ready to challenge Barbara's enemies at court, of whom there were more than a few. She had every desire to be a lady of the bedchamber, and he had no intention of thwarting her. Clarendon was told to inform the queen that this would be the case, and that his majesty would brook no opposition. Much as he disliked Barbara himself, he had no choice but to obey orders. With sympathy and a heavy heart, he implored her to give in gracefully, stressing that she need not have such little confidence in herself that she should feel threatened by another woman, and that as a wife it was her duty to submit to her husband's commands. Over the course of several meetings, she insisted tearfully that while the king might do what he pleased, she could not consent to it.

At one point, she withdrew from spending any more time with the king than was strictly necessary, and in a heated moment she declared that she would sooner return to her old home in Portugal than openly accept such a humiliating state of affairs in a foreign land where she was obviously not wanted. The king retaliated by dismissing most of the servants who had accompanied her from Portugal, and allowing Barbara to make a home for herself at Hampton Court. Maintaining his remarkable insensitivity, he brought her into the queen's presence as a matter of daily routine, carrying on conversation with her and taking little notice of his wife.

The latter was humiliatingly excluded from court entertainments and treated with scant respect by some of her English servants, who were quick to notice that she was being treated as a cipher and therefore of little importance. When Henrietta Maria, the queen mother, left France and arrived at the English court, Queen Catherine hoped that she might have an influential ally, especially as she was also a Roman Catholic and might have been expected to bring some influence to bear on her son with regard to his marriage vows and a simple matter of respect. Instead, the queen mother proved no help at all. She seemed quite unconcerned and all she could do was try to persuade Catherine that she would have to make the best of the situation. Far from spurning her son's mistress, she accepted his stance and readily acknowledged the countess of Castlemaine in public.

All the queen could do was to accept Barbara with good if reluctant grace. The latter intended to fulfil her duties as conspicuously as she could. Catherine had to take what comfort she could in the fact that she was a queen consort while Barbara was little more than a mere servant. She might be a remarkably privileged one, yet she was at the mercy of an unpredictable master who might tire of her at any time, although he would be certain to let her down gently and was unlikely to treat her badly.

What added greatly to her sadness was that Catherine did the best she could to fulfil the primary purpose of a queen consort. She soon became pregnant—and did so three times altogether during the next few years. Yet she never managed to carry a living child to full term. In 1662, she had a miscarriage. The following year she was seriously ill, and for a while she was convinced that she had indeed given birth to a living child. With questionable tact, Charles tried to offer her some comfort by telling her she had just delivered two sons and a daughter. Her misery on learning a little later that she had done no such thing after suffering for several weeks can only be imagined. Further pregnancies in February 1666, in May 1668, and again in June 1669 each resulted in the birth of a stillborn child.[3] Being a married man did nothing to make him change his ways, and he continued to have children by his many mistresses, which in view of her obstetric difficulties she must have found galling in the extreme as a constant reminder of the shortcomings over which she had no control.

In spite of this, he insisted that she should be treated with respect by other people—a rule from which, judging by the way he had introduced her and Barbara with an unwarranted baptism of fire, he evidently believed himself exempt. There are those who say that he later sided with her against his mistresses when he felt that she was not receiving the courtesy due to her, so perhaps he had learned a lesson after all. But that is open to speculation.

After the miscarriages, it was increasingly obvious that Queen Catherine was never going to bear an heir. Royal advisers urged the monarch to seek a divorce, hoping that the new wife would be fertile and also Protestant, but Charles had sufficient loyalty to her to refuse to consider what might have been called 'the Henry VIII solution'. There was no talk of annulling the marriage, let alone any whispers of treason that might have led to a spell in the Tower of London or even worse.

Catherine must have been grateful that her infertility did not endanger her status as queen, even though it was beyond her control. If Charles had chosen to divorce her on whatever grounds he chose, he could have remarried and had an heir as soon as he wanted. His ever-growing brood of children born on the wrong side of the blanket was adequate confirmation that the problem was nothing to do with him. Alternatively, if his conscience, or lack of a marriage certificate between himself and Lucy Barlow, did not permit him to swear a solemn and binding oath to declare that his son, James, was legitimate, he could have declared his legitimacy by Act of Parliament; or he could have pronounced that bastardy did not prevent him from inheriting the crown. There were also grounds for supposing that, as the eldest son of King Charles, if he succeeded to the crown, his bastardy would be automatically cancelled.[4]

*****

Of all the illegitimate children of King Charles II, the figure of James Scott looms the largest. Not only was he the firstborn, but also the one whose life is best documented, the only one who ever sought to claim the crown after his father had died (a distinction only to be expected of the eldest, despite the unusual circumstances), and the only one to suffer the same fate as his paternal grandfather in ending his life on the scaffold.

He was brought to England at the age of thirteen, and in February 1663, he was made duke of Monmouth, with the subsidiary titles of earl of Doncaster and Baron Scott of Tynedale. One month later, he was appointed Knight of the Garter. On 20 April, a few days after his fourteenth birthday, he married Anne Scott, duchess of Buccleuch, and he took his wife's surname upon marriage. Gossips at court whispered that the date of his marriage, which had been planned for some time, was brought forward as Barbara Villiers had taken more than a passing fancy to him. On the following day, he was made duke of Buccleuch, and the couple also received the titles of earl and countess of Dalkeith, and Lord and Lady Scott of Whitchester and Eskdale in the Peerage of Scotland. Observers found him a charming youth, although restless and perpetually on the move. At sixteen, Pepys thought him 'the most skittish leaping gallant that I ever saw, always in action, vaulting or leaping, or clambering'.[5]

Like father, like son. Being a married man did not prevent Monmouth from having mistresses and additional children, though on a lesser scale than the king. A relationship with Eleanor, daughter of Sir Robert Needham, a member of parliament during the Civil War, resulted in the birth of a son, James, and two daughters, Henrietta and Isabel, the latter dying young (although she was the namesake of one of King Charles II's short-term mistresses, they were apparently unrelated). In his last months, he had a second, Henrietta, Baroness Wentworth, although they had no children together.

It had been accepted since the Restoration that James, duke of York, was his brother's heir to the throne until such time as Charles married and had heirs of his own. The duke of Monmouth was not King Charles's heir, and because of his illegitimacy, he was barred from the succession, unless his father chose to take steps to have this altered. It was theoretically in his power, and moreover, it would have met a degree of approval. At about this time there was a movement among the Parliamentarians to prevent the duke of York from succeeding, as he was seen as an inflexible Catholic with his father's obstinacy and none of his brother's *laissez-faire*.

King Charles was fond of his eldest son, but accepted without question that as a bastard he could not possibly come to the throne. Although he had his personal differences with his brother and would do so for the rest of his life, he stopped short of depriving him of his birthright. This did nothing to prevent rumours that he planned to make the boy his heir, especially when the latter seemed anxious to give the impression that his parents had been married. The king apparently did nothing to discourage his presumption, and regularly showered him with honours. In any case, Monmouth's defenders could always cite the precedent of William of Normandy's bastardy, admittedly almost six centuries earlier in a very different age. Being born out of wedlock had not prevented the duke of Normandy from landing in England and taking the crown by conquest.

Circumstances might have altered considerably since 1066, but father and son were still comparatively young. Time was on Monmouth's side, and he knew well enough to keep to himself the ambitions that would have only created dissent between his father and himself. As he became older, more self-confident, and more open to being led astray by others, he would sail into dangerous waters. Yet at this stage, loyalty and a united dynasty were the best assurance for the stability of the monarchy that might still be regarded as those of a republican inclination on probation.

The duke, still only a boy of sixteen, was not one to shirk the duty of serving his country. He cheerfully took his place in the English fleet in the Second Anglo-Dutch War in 1665, and he saw action at the inconclusive Battle of Solebay off the coast of Suffolk. Regarded as a courageous fighter, in June 1666, he returned to England and was appointed captain of a troop of cavalry. In September 1668, he was made colonel of the His Majesty's Own Troop of Horse Guards. Nearly two years later, in May 1670, he acquired Moor Park in Hertfordshire when Josceline Percy, earl of Northumberland, died without leaving a male heir, the estate reverted to the crown, and it was presented by the king to Monmouth. This was one prize granted to him that would soon slip from his grasp as the countess of Northumberland successfully sued for the estates to be returned to the late earl's only daughter and sole heiress, Lady Elizabeth Percy. There were limits to even the power of King Charles.

At the outbreak of the Third Anglo-Dutch War in 1672, a brigade of 6,000 English and Scottish troops was sent to serve as part of the French army (in return for money paid to King Charles), with Monmouth as its commander. He became lord lieutenant of the East Riding in Yorkshire and governor of Kingston-upon-Hull in April 1673. In a campaign in the Low Countries later that year, and in particular at the Siege of Maastricht that June, his bravery under fire was praised, not least by King Louis XIV. In 1674, he became chancellor of Cambridge University and master of the horse, and King Charles II directed that all military orders should be brought first to Monmouth for examination, thus giving him effective command of the forces, with responsibilities including the movement of troops and the suppression of riots. In March 1677, he also became lord lieutenant of Staffordshire. Under the protectorship of his devoted father, as long as he conducted himself properly, he had nothing to fear.

Having known gracious living and then hardship in her earlier years, once Barbara, countess of Castlemaine, was raised to the unofficial status of his majesty's chief mistress, or as some would cynically call her behind her back, 'the uncrowned queen', she was determined to make the most of her good fortune, in more ways than one. John Evelyn was unimpressed with her, writing of how he 'also saw that famous beauty, but in my opinion of a childish, simple, and baby face'. Not long afterwards, he was calling her a 'another lady of pleasure and curse of our nation'.[6] Her regal lover could evidently refuse her nothing, and was said to have granted her lavish pensions and regular income from various sources of government revenue, in addition to paying off her debts as necessary. She was said to have won £25,000 on cards in a single night, and lost £15,000 on another.[7]

In addition to her remarkable extravagance and perpetual promiscuity, she had a temper that did not spare the king when she was displeased. She held influence over him in her position as royal mistress, and in addition to receiving a generous allowance from the king, she helped herself to money from the Privy Purse as well as taking bribes from the Spanish and the

French. He was considered by those who surrounded them to be besotted with her, and unable to refuse her anything within reason. Although widely disliked, she had her redeeming qualities. Some people at court testified to her being good company, keeping an excellent table, and with a generous heart to compensate for the fiery temper. It was also observed once that after a scaffold had fallen onto a crowd of people at the theatre, she rushed to assist an injured child, something that few other ladies of the court might have bothered with.

Nevertheless, she had enemies in high places. The earl of Clarendon, who next to the king was probably the most important man at court, was foremost among those who distrusted her. From the moment he realised that she was attaching herself to the king, he foresaw that with her reputation for being flighty, extravagant, and headstrong, she would cause trouble for those around her. She quickly sensed his attitude towards her and made a point of forming friendships with his opponents, as a convenient way of getting rid of him once he fell from favour. Defeats in the Anglo-Dutch War from 1665 onwards, the disasters of the Great Plague in England of 1665, and the Great Fire of London a year later, combined with his failing health, made it easier for his foes in government to suggest to the king that his resignation should be sought. When he left Whitehall for the last time, the countess could not conceal her delight at the removal of an awkward presence.

The countess of Castlemaine's appointment as lady of the bedchamber was followed by rumours of an estrangement between her and the king, the result of his infatuation with another woman who was not his wife. Frances Stuart, a prominent member of the court of the Restoration, held out firmly against her sovereign's desires and refused to become his mistress. The daughter of Walter Stuart, a physician in the court of Queen Henrietta Maria, and a distant relative of the royal family, and his wife, Sophia, she had been born on 8 July 1647 in exile in Paris. Henrietta Maria sent her to England when she was sixteen years old to be a maid of honour and later a lady-in-waiting to Queen Catherine. Samuel Pepys called her one of the greatest beauties he had ever seen, and she had several suitors. However, she had a reputation for not being particularly clever, something that in such an age might have been regarded as an advantage. Some spoke of her as being childish and silly, and count de Grammont once said slightingly of her that 'it would be difficult to imagine less brain combined with more beauty'.[8]

As a member of the royal court, Frances caught the eye of King Charles, and he was instantly smitten with her. An inveterate gossip, she was always ready to pass on information about others and laugh at his jokes. He was soon so infatuated with her that when the queen's life was despaired of in 1663, it was rumoured that he was planning to marry her, and four years later after the queen recovered, he was considering the possibility of obtaining a divorce to enable him to make her his wife as she had refused to become his mistress. If this is true, perhaps she was not quite the fool that some made her out to be.

In March 1667, she married (thus becoming the third wife of) Charles Stuart, duke of Richmond and duke of Lennox, a fourth cousin of King Charles II. It was rumoured that she had to elope, after being discovered with him in a compromising situation by Barbara. Now duchess of Richmond, she remained at court for many years, and although an attack of smallpox in 1669 did no favours to her good looks, through tactful behaviour and personality she remained on excellent terms with the fickle king. Her married life was a short one, for her husband's career as ambassador firstly to Scotland and then to Denmark ended when he drowned at Elsinore in 1672, leaving no children by any of his wives. A belief persisted that the king had had him sent to appointments abroad without his wife, so that he himself would have the pleasure of her company at home.

Despite the king being thoroughly besotted by the duchess of Richmond for a brief spell, Barbara remained relatively secure in the king's affections, or at least secure at court. Both had other lovers, to the extent that it was if each was leading an open marriage in all but name, with several partners and no marriage certificates to prove anything more than an intense mutual infatuation. In the free and easy moral climate of the Stuart Court, Barbara and Charles were mutually attracted by lust if not by love. They knew they needed each other, and she had a powerful hold over him, as well as a stormy temper when she was thwarted. A feeling persists that she was the more dominant character of the two, and for some years he could refuse her nothing, while always ready to carry on with other women when she was not around. Yet it is supposed that quite a strong affection must have bound them both together for a few years.

In December 1663, Barbara announced that she was converting from Anglicanism to Roman Catholicism. Historians disagree as to why she did so. Some believe it was an attempt to consolidate her position with the king, who was a Roman Catholic himself—if not a particularly devout one—and others a way of strengthening her ties with her Catholic husband. The king seemed quite unconcerned, saying that he was interested in ladies' bodies, but not their souls, while the court generally took the view that the Church of Rome had gained nothing by her conversion and the Church of England had lost nothing.

The last of the countess of Castlemaine's children that can be said with certainty to have fathered by King Charles was their third son, George, born in December 1665. By this time, perhaps having had too much of her grasping and domineering ways, he was beginning to find her company less enjoyable than before. Yet there would be no sudden end to the favours that she was receiving from him. In June 1670, he created her Baroness Nonsuch, as she was the owner of Nonsuch Palace, near Epsom and Ewell. At the same time, she was also briefly granted the ownership of Phoenix Park in Dublin as a present from the king and made countess of Castlemaine and duchess of Cleveland in her own right. Some at court wondered if this indicated that she was about to be sidelined by Charles after receiving what could have been seen as a farewell present or, in modern colloquial terms, a golden handshake or 'pay-off'. The title was conferred on her with a special remainder that allowed it to be passed to her eldest son, Charles Fitzroy, despite his illegitimacy.

Once the third son was born, the association between Charles and Barbara continued for some time, but his ardour had evidently cooled. He sought his pleasures of the flesh elsewhere, with several mistresses in turn. Some of them were reluctant to respond, and he did not succeed in bedding every one of them. In 1667, Pepys, in conversation with Evelyn, could speak of King Charles as a man who 'never was known to keep two mistresses in his life', in other words, at the same time.[9] Within a few years, he was clearly keeping at least two, almost certainly more, at a time. They included Winifred Wells, one of Queen Catherine's maids of honour; Mrs Jane Roberts, the daughter of a clergyman; Mrs Knight, a singer whose voice was greatly admired at court; and two more members of the nobility, Mary Bagot, countess of Falmouth, whose first husband had been killed at the Battle of Lowestoft in 1665 during the war with Holland, and Elizabeth, countess of Kildare. There were others who were shown secretly upstairs at night by the king's confidential servants, and whose names would remain unrecorded.

*****

Charles Palmer, later Charles Fitzroy, the eldest son of Barbara, bore only one courtesy title, that of Lord Limerick, until 1670. That year, he was made earl of Southampton. He was installed Knight of the Garter on 1 April 1673 and duke of Southampton, earl of Chichester, and Baron Newbury on 10 September 1675.

The same year he received his first earldom, at the age of eight, he was betrothed to Mary Wood, who was one year younger than him. It would be of great financial advantage to him, for she was the only child and sole heiress of Sir Henry Wood, clerk of the green cloth, and heir to £4,000 *per annum*. The arrangement was on condition that the marriage would be delayed until Mary had reached the age of sixteen. After the death of Sir Henry on 25 May 1671, Mary went to live with her aunt, Lady Chester, but the countess of Castlemaine had her abducted and married to the nine-year-old Southampton, demanding that the girl who would become her daughter-in-law should be brought up with her daughters. Lady Chester protested, but to no avail. The wedding ceremony was repeated when the couple were of full age in 1677.

George Fitzroy, the third and youngest son of Charles and Barbara, was born in 'a fellow's chamber' at Merton College, Oxford, on 28 December 1665. On New Year's Day 1666, he was baptised according to an entry made by Antony Wood in the register of the parish of St John the Baptist, Oxford, as 'George Palmer, sonne of Roger, earl of Castlemaine'. After the name of his mother, the entry concluded, '*Filius naturalis regis Caroli II*'. A private copy of the register makes reference to 'George Palmer, base son of King Charles II'.

The good people of Oxford had apparently been scandalised by the mother coming to give birth to the king's child in their community, and Wood referred in his diary to a 'libell on the countess of Castlemayne's dore in Merton College' one day in January. It suggested that if the child had not been the son of King Charles, the mother would have been 'ducked', said to be the contemporary Oxford method of 'dealing with undesirable ladies'. The sum of £1,000 was offered as a reward for the discovery of the libel's author, but it did not lead to the party responsible. Nevertheless, the furore did not bother the countess of Castlemaine, who shrugged it off and said with pride that her son was born 'among the scholars'.[10]

Mindful of the caprices of fate, Barbara was determined that her sons should be well-provided for financially. Their semi-royal status was no guarantee of security, and nothing was to be taken for granted. A sound education would also be important. In September 1674, she visited Oxford University and spoke to Dr John Fell, bishop of Oxford, asking him if he would take Charles into his care. She felt he needed a firm upbringing, as he compared unfavourably with his youngest brother, George, who was 'far more apt to receive instructions than his elder brother, whom she confesseth to be a very kockish [*sic*] idle boy'.[11]

George duly enrolled, but without any great show of enthusiasm on the part of those who would be in charge of his studies. Humphrey Prideaux, dean of Christ Church, noted in November in a letter to his friend John Ellis, an under-secretary of state, that Harry Aldrich had been appointed his tutor: 'what he will get by him I know not. It is the general desire among us that he come not'.[12]

He matriculated at Christ Church, Oxford, in December 1675, but those who knew him well could see that he was never going to be an intellectual, or even in the least clever. Prideaux, who had come to like him but could readily see his shortcomings, wrote in October 1676 that his young charge was 'kept very orderly, but will ever be very simple, and scarce, I believe, ever attain to the reputation of not being a fool'.[13] The children of King Charles and the countess were considered to be lacking in intelligence, and were popularly referred to as 'the blockheads'.[14] It was decided that both boys should spend some time travelling in Europe to broaden their horizons, and the task of supervising them fell to Professor Edward Bernard. After a while, he had had enough of them and especially their mother, according to Prideaux:

> My friend Mr Bernard, who went into France to attend upon the two bastards of Cleveland, hath been so affronted and abused there by that insolent woman that he hath been forced to quit that employment and return.[15]

Henry Fitzroy, the second son, was born on 28 September 1663 (although some sources suggest it was a few weeks earlier) at his mother's house in King Street, near Whitehall Palace. Suspecting doubts as to his paternity, the king was a little slow in acknowledging the boy as one of his own, but by the time he was about eight, he could see the family resemblance. He certainly seemed to develop a fondness for him as a baby, and there is a charming picture left by an anonymous observer of how the king 'goes at midnight to her [Barbara's] nurses and takes her child up and dances it in his arms—the child being the five-months-old Henry, whom he thus treats kindly, in spite of not yet accepting him as his own offspring'.[16]

Charlotte Lee, countess of Lichfield, born Lady Charlotte Fitzroy on 5 September 1664 at Whitehall Palace, was the second daughter of Barbara and King Charles. She was placed in the care of a governess in Berkshire House, St James's. Once the king acknowledged her, she bore the surname of Fitzroy, 'child of the King'. Pepys assumed that her marriage prospects were likely to be good: 'my Lady Castlemaine will in merriment say that her daughter, not above a year old or two, will be the first maid in the Court that will be married'.[17] For want of anything else to record, the historian John Heneage Jesse wrote of her: 'we know but little of her except that she was beautiful'.[18] As a child, she was painted by Lely, seated with her Indian page, holding a bunch of grapes and dressed in pink silk. The art historian Anna Brownell Jameson described her as having 'rivalled her mother in beauty, but was far unlike her in every other respect'.[19]

On 16 May 1674, before her tenth birthday, she was contracted to marry Sir Edward Lee, who was created 1st earl of Lichfield. They were married on 6 February 1677, in her thirteenth year. Her dowry was agreed at £18,000, and her husband was awarded a pension of £2,000 per year.

King Charles II appears to have been a loving father to most, if not all, of his children, and he was pleased to hear about any grandchildren that were on their way. In 1682, he wrote to Charlotte: 'I must tell you I am glad to hear you are with child, and I hope to see you here before it be long, that I may have the satisfaction myself of telling you how much I love you, and how truly I am your kind father, Charles Rex.'[20] She was spoken of as being particularly gentle-natured, and some thought that her character had benefited from her being removed from her mother's care at a relatively early age. Her uncle, the duke of York, was also very fond of her, appreciated her intelligence, and frequently wrote to her on family matters and public affairs.

The paternity of the countess of Castlemaine's two youngest daughters was open to doubt. Cecilia, born in 1670 or 1671 or possibly as early as 1668, was indisputably her child, but more likely to have been fathered by Henry Jermyn, an associate of the duke of York with whom she had become friendly. This was almost certainly the child whose paternity was questioned by the king while she was pregnant. He was particularly angry with her for having been carrying on with Jermyn, and he told her he himself had not lain with her for months. She allegedly retorted, 'God damn me, but you shall own it', and give it the family name of Fitzroy: 'she should have it christened in the Chapel Royal, and owned as his, or otherwise she would bring it to the gallery in Whitehall, and dash its brains out before his face'.[21,22]

By any standards, it was an extraordinary remark for an expectant mother to make. She was slow to forgive him, and the quarrel was not settled for another three weeks or so. She retired in high dudgeon to stay at a house in Covent Garden, owned by Sir Daniel Harvey, whose wife Elizabeth was a mistress of the duke of York. The king came to visit her, and according to Pepys, 'she made him ask her forgiveness upon his knees, and promise to offend her no more so, and that indeed, she did threaten to bring all his bastards to his closet door and hath nearly hectored him out of his wits'.[23]

Little is known about the later life of Cecilia beyond that she never married, was said to be an excellent musician and avid collector of books, entered the Benedictine monastery at Dunkirk in about 1713, and died there in 1759. This indicates that she lived into her late eighties. In view of the fact that none of Charles II's other illegitimate children reached the age of seventy, it is considered that this is a further reason for suggesting that he may not have been her father after all.

The same seems true of Barbara, born in 1672 and named after her mother. The child claimed that she was the daughter of King Charles, but she was more likely to be the daughter of John Churchill, later duke of Marlborough. Lord Castlemaine allegedly believed her to be his daughter, but this seems unlikely as husband and wife had been unofficially separated for a long time by the time she was born. In spite of this, on his death in 1705, he still bequeathed her his estate.

Apart from two London actresses and a Frenchwoman of aristocratic origins, there would be more mistresses who held sway but briefly, and without presenting him with additional sons and daughters. Between them there was a certain amount of rivalry, sometimes friendly but sometimes not, between each member of the triumvirate, and the first of these relationships was to be the shortest.

*****

Mary Davis was born in Westminster around 1648 and thought to be the illegitimate child of either Thomas Howard, 3rd earl of Berkshire, or his elder brother Charles, or according to other sources of an unnamed blacksmith from Wiltshire. In 1663, she became a professional actress in the Duke's Theatre Company, one of two organisations chartered by King Charles just after the Restoration when the theatres reopened following the interregnum and a return to normality. As a popular singer, dancer, and comedian, she adopted the forename of Moll, and was afterwards always known thus. She met the king in a theatre or a coffeehouse in 1667 and became his mistress soon afterwards.

At the start of the relationship, she was said to be fairly quiet, even diffident, but she apparently gained rapidly in confidence. Having reached such an exalted role, she was considered by others quite shameless in flaunting the wealth she acquired from her close association with the king, and soon gained a reputation for vulgarity and greed. Proud of the presents and money he showered upon her, she enjoyed showing off her 'mighty pretty fine coach' and a very expensive ring. Samuel Pepys was impressed with her, although his wife Elizabeth begged to differ and called her 'the most impertinent slut in the world'.[24]

This view was not hers alone, for Moll was said to be not outstandingly pretty but possessed of a powerful singing voice, had excellent legs, and a 'suggestive dancing style' that appealed to the king, but so revolted the queen that after seeing at least one of her performances she walked out of the theatre in disgust. During one production at court one night in May 1668, Moll was required to dance a jig. When she got up to do so, Queen Catherine left at once. This was at a time, Pepys noted, when the countess of Castlemaine found herself very much out of favour at the same time, 'the King coming little to her, and thus she [is] mighty melancholy and discontented'.[25]

In 1668, Moll put the stage career behind her, perhaps because as a result of the king's generosity she no longer needed to work so hard for a living. Her relationship with him seemed to be a casual one, although she gave him another daughter, named Mary, on 16 October 1673. One or two sources suggest 1668, and if the latter date is correct, she was almost certainly the last of the children that King Charles admitted was his. As a reference to their collateral descent from the Tudor family, little Mary was given the name Lady Mary Tudor on being acknowledged by her father in December 1680, granted a warrant of precedency as the daughter of an earl, and in 1683 as daughter of a duke. At this stage, she was granted an annuity of £1,500, paid in four instalments, the final payment being made in 1687 as a gift for her wedding.

Shortly after the confinement, Charles and Moll went their different ways, presumably as their affair had run its course. Nevertheless, when he ended their association, he awarded her an annual pension for life of £1,000.

*****

The countess of Castlemaine probably knew enough about the king's character, and she had the foresight to realise that her unofficial position as 'The King's Mistress' was no sinecure and could not be taken for granted. Keen to do what she reasonably could for her children and ensure that they would not want for money, she was anxious to try and provide for suitable marriages for them. It was largely down to her matchmaking that in August 1672 her second son, Henry, was promised in marriage to five-year-old Isabella, daughter and heiress of Henry Bennet, 1st earl of Arlington. The betrothal was confirmed by a formal ceremony at which the archbishop of Canterbury, Gilbert Sheldon, officiated, 'the King and all the grandees being present'. John Evelyn, who was also there, commented on Isabella, 'a sweet child if ever there was any,' but he 'took no great joy at the thing for many reasons'.[26] Three weeks later, the young husband-to-be was made earl of Euston, after Arlington's house in Suffolk, and on 11 September 1675, he also became duke of Grafton, the title by which he would generally be known and remembered.

Barbara knew it would be only sensible for her to take as much as possible as she could from the king (and from the exchequer) while she held sway as 'the royal whore' before he tired of her and found another to take her place, in order to ensure that she could live in comfort for the rest of her days. At the same time, it was shrewd of her to find herself lovers elsewhere, such as Henry Jermyn, 1st Baron Dover, the acrobat Jacob Hall, and in particular her second cousin, John Churchill. The latter had the good sense to take financial advantage of her favours while he could, and he bought himself an annuity with the £5,000 with which she presented him.

King Charles was not bothered when he heard that she was transferring her affections elsewhere, and he was amused to learn about the annuity. He remarked that, after all, a young man must have something to live on. Moreover, with his wandering eye, he was also looking elsewhere. As early as 1667, Pepys had heard gossip about a proposed pension to pay her off; she was 'as high as ever she was', though the king was 'as weary as possible, and would give anything to remove her; but he is so weak in his passion that he dared not do it'.[27] Wearisome she might be, but those who were closest to him suspected that he quailed before the thought of another of her bursts of bad temper.

It would be affairs of state that culminated in the end of her privileged position, albeit a few years later. Most of those at court were able to accept or at least tolerate her unashamed promiscuity and extravagant spending which were meat and drink to the satirists, who enjoyed making fun of the king and his entourage. Yet the position of royal mistress was a precarious one, and she had not been worried about making enemies.

In the end it was the Test Act, passed in 1673 to ban Catholics from holding office, that made her position no longer tenable and ended her employment as lady of the bedchamber. By this time, she had thoroughly outstayed her welcome, was no longer indispensable to her former protector, and had long since been supplanted as his mistress—not by one, not by two, but in fact by three women. She departed from court, as she had no choice to do anything else, with the words echoing in her ears from her sovereign to go and live quietly, cause no scandal, and if she behaved herself, he would not care whom she loved.

The name of Nell Gwyn, or Eleanor to give her her true birth name, has come down to posterity as by far the best-known of King Charles II's mistresses. During her lifetime, she was easily the most popular, perhaps because of her 'low birth' and lack of aristocratic blood. What is known of her personality suggests that she was a likeable, unpretentious, warm-hearted young woman totally lacking in arrogance, self-assertive if the occasion demanded, yet with no desire to push herself forward, demand exceptional favours, or make enemies.

Her early years were shrouded in mystery, with some doubt as to whether she was born in London, Hereford, or Oxford, although the first appears the most probable. Even her date of birth is open to dispute, with the majority of sources agreeing on 2 February 1650 or thereabouts, while others suggest it was sometime in 1642. Her father deserted his wife and two daughters when the latter were very small, and her mother, Helena, was an alcoholic who spent her life in the West End of London. To try and make ends meet, she ran a brothel in which one or both children, Nell and Rose, may have worked as child prostitutes. Like Moll Davis, in her adult years, she initially worked in the theatre before coming to the attention of King Charles. She and Rose were initially employed as 'orange girls' to sell fruits to members of the audience inside the theatre, and for tips to pass messages between theatregoers and audiences backstage, usually regarding secret assignations afterwards. By 1665, if not earlier, she was appearing onstage.

Two years later, George Villiers, 2nd duke of Buckingham, took on the role of unofficial manager for Gwyn's love affairs. He was trying to provide the king with someone to take the place of the countess of Castlemaine, as their relationship was clearly beginning to cool. Buckingham was one of the most flamboyant characters at court, and he could reduce the king to helpless laughter with his mimicry, but he was generally regarded as unreliable and untrustworthy. Although he was a cousin of Barbara, they were not at all close to each other, and he was ready to try and find someone to replace her where the monarch's physical needs were concerned. Nell was tempted, as would be any young woman in such circumstances, but reportedly asked £500 a year to be maintained in comfort, a sum that was considered too dear. Instead, Buckingham came to an arrangement to set the king up with Moll Davis instead. Both women would become rivals, and while Nell was not yet prepared to commit herself fully, she became something of a rival to her fellow actress. Both women became friends to an extent, although they could not resist the temptation to play pranks on each other. The story is often told that Nell invited Moll to tea one day, shortly before the latter had arranged to spend an evening with the king in bed, having slyly added a laxative to her cakes beforehand.

Around April 1668, she was attending a performance at the Lincoln's Inn Fields theatre and was in a box adjacent to the king. It was probably not the first time they had met, and they seemed to spend more time flirting with each other that night than watching the play. Afterwards he invited her and her escort to take supper with him and the duke of York. When they had finished eating and the time came to settle up their bill, the king declared he had no money or him, and neither did his brother. Nell therefore had to pay, remarking in imitation of what was evidently one of the king's favourite expressions, 'Oddsfish, but this is the poorest company I ever was in!'[28]

Having been born into a poverty-stricken childhood and then known what it was like to work for her living, she had made up her mind that, if possible, she would never want for money again as long as she lived. Having suggested a price to the king for her personal services that he had rejected, she found a new lover who was prepared to pay her £100 a year less than she had suggested to his majesty. The man who had obtained her at a discount was the wit, poet, and courtier Charles Sackville, Lord Buckhurst, later 6th earl of Dorset. He soon wearied of her constant demands for more money, and she accordingly took up with the actor Charles Hart. This coupling did not last long, and for a while he found his pleasures in the company and bed of the countess of Castlemaine, Meanwhile, Nell, who had perhaps learnt by now to moderate her financial demands more realistically, henceforth attached herself to the king, or the man she now jokingly called 'her Charles the Third'.

By mid-1668, their affair was well-known, though there was little reason to believe it would last for long. She continued to act at the King's House, her new notoriety drawing larger crowds and encouraging the playwrights to craft more roles specifically for her. As her commitment to the king increased, she took on less acting roles. She became a regular visitor to the king's private bedroom. One morning he pretended he was unwell, as he wanted to spend some more time in bed with her. Wanting to see how he was, Queen Catherine came to see him. There was only just enough advance warning for Nell to get out of bed in her nightgown and conceal herself behind the wall hangings. Too late did she realise that she had left one of her slippers beside the bed. When the queen arrived and saw it, she excused herself, saying she had better not stay, otherwise 'the pretty fool' that owned it might catch cold.

During her first years with the king, there was little competition in the way of other mistresses. Barbara Palmer's days as *maitresse en titre* were evidently now numbered. The only other contender was the less outgoing Moll Davis, who kept quietly away from the spotlight of public appearances or Whitehall. However, she was not always the shrinking violet. On a visit with King Charles to the races at Newmarket, a Colonel Abercromby spoke disrespectfully to her, and she challenged him to a duel. He accepted, she dressed herself in men's clothes, they fought together, and she wounded him in the left shoulder. Clearly beaten, he apologised or offered to 'compose the quarrel' and to pay her 100 guineas as compensation.[29] She had been unaware that the king was watching, and afterwards he commended her for her bravery. Her defeated opponent henceforth retired from public life.

Moll was said to put on a rather better performance on stage than Nell Gwyn. The latter must have noticed praise and compliments being showered on her, and not without a hint of envy; Pepys, for one, said her dancing was 'infinitely beyond' that of a similar recent performance from the former orange girl. Moll was thus doubtless regarded as an unwelcome rival. It was said that Nell invited her to tea one day, just before she was due to leave for an intimate assignation in the king's chamber. She offered her guest not only tea, but also a slice of cake to which she had added some jalap, a powerful laxative.

By the autumn of 1669, Nell was expecting a child, and at her house in Lincoln's Inn Fields, she gave birth to a boy, on 8 May. He was the king's seventh son, by five separate mistresses. She had decided to name him Charles after his father, thus making him the king's Charles the Fourth. For the next few days, while recovering from the birth, she adopted the custom of 'upsitting', and during the next few days her bedchamber became a salon for visitors who came to wish her well. One of them was John Dryden, an admirer of hers who told her he was keen to see her back on the stage before long.

During the years to come, little Charles would have a special place in his father's heart. If the duke of Monmouth was his favourite son until he tried his patience too many times in later years, Nell's firstborn was surely the second. Ironically, by this time, it was noticed that he seemed to be taking less interest in the birth of yet another child, who at first seemed to occupy his thoughts but little. He remained as pleasure-loving as ever, and after having survived on the throne for ten years without any serious crises, seemed content to leave the governance of the country to others.

Moreover, the new arrival coincided with one of his infrequent ventures into national diplomacy. He had long been keen to establish a closer relationship with France, a country he viewed as a natural ally, and the previous year he had declared that he intended to enter the Roman

Catholic Church and bring England back to the same faith. Fortunately, he lacked the duke of York's dogmatism and proved successful at concealing his aims to a degree from a nation that viewed papism with deep suspicion.

His sister, Henriette-Anne, always known within the family as 'Minette', was unhappily married to Philippe, duc d'Orleans, the gay brother of King Louis XIV. She was determined to visit England again, and Louis encouraged her to go to England in order to help cement the Treaty of Dover, thus affirming an alliance with France in her ongoing war with the Dutch Republic. As it was realised that such a move would be unpopular in England, the signing and terms of the 'secret treaty' remained unknown to all but a select few for over a century. Minette came to stay with her brother, with neither knowing it would be the last time they would meet. Having suffered ill-health since childhood, she had been afflicted by digestive complaints for a few years. Less than two weeks after she returned to France in June 1670, she became ill and died of peritonitis from a ruptured ulcer, although as she lay dying, she cried out in agony that she had been poisoned. Her death left King Charles and James, duke of York, the only surviving siblings, and the king was heartbroken.

On her deathbed, Minette had made a special request that her brother should help all her poor servants as much as he possibly could. One of her ladies, Henriette de Bordes, who had been with Minette on her deathbed, was given a post in England as chief dresser to Queen Catherine. A few months later, she was joined by another, Louise de Kérouaille, who was also to be a maid of honour to Queen Catherine. It did not take the others at court long to notice that Charles was attracted to her, although her close connection with his beloved sister may have played a part in this.

Nell returned briefly to the stage later in 1670, but the following year would witness her last season of a seven-year career in the theatre. In February 1671, she moved into a new house at 79 Pall Mall, and it would be her main residence for the rest of her life. Within a few weeks, she was expecting a second child by the king, and another son was born on 25 December, named James. The king granted Nell and their son a house, renamed Burford House, at Home Park, Windsor, and she lived there when he was in residence at the castle. She also had a summer residence in central London, where she entertained Charles II with little concerts and breakfasts. An inscribed stone of 1680, saved and reinserted in the front wall of the present building, shows a carved mask, probably a reference to her stage career.

On 21 December 1676, a warrant was passed for 'a grant to Charles Beauclerk, and to the heirs male of his body, of the dignities of Baron of Headington, Oxford, and Earl of Burford in the same county, with remainder to his brother, James Beauclerk, and the heirs male of his body'. A few weeks later, James was given 'the title of Lord Beauclerk, with the place and precedence of the eldest son of an earl'.

Two stories, both possibly no more than that, describe how Nell's sons, or at least the elder, came to be granted titles. It had long rankled with her that the sons of the countess of Castlemaine had titles, the duchess of Portsmouth's son had been ennobled at the age of only three, and hers still did not. The first is that when Charles was playing in the nursery the king asked to see him, and his mother called, 'Come here, you little bastard, and greet your father.' When the king rebuked her for calling him thus, she replied that his majesty has given him no other name by which to call him. Realising that he had overlooked the simple matter of granting his little son a title, he created him earl of Burford. Another tale would have us believe that she held him out of a window of the house (or above a river) and threatened to drop him unless he was given a peerage. Charles supposedly cried out 'God save the Earl of Burford!' and subsequently bestowed the name on him officially. Beauclerk, or Beauclerc, was an old French name, meaning a steward, fine penmanship, and an interest in learning. It had been bestowed by medieval chroniclers on King Henry I of England as he was supposed to have been well educated, although more modern historians have disputed this as probably fiction. Why it was chosen in this instance is not known, apart from the fact that King Charles evidently wanted to choose something different from the growing ranks of Fitzroys, in order to save confusion.

At a young age, the younger Charles was said to identify himself as being the king's son. He accompanied his father on visits to the royal guards or on inspections of the naval fleet, and he was inspired by tales and recollections from his half-brother, the duke of Monmouth, and also Prince Rupert of the Rhine, Charles II's cousin and a veteran of the Civil War, of heroism on the battlefield. All three felt the young boy showed great promise, fostering his interest in military matters. From an early age, he seemed primed for a career in the English forces. When he was about six, Nell chose as his tutor Fleetwood Sheppard, who had been a steward in her household and also responsible for her financial affairs. Fleetwood was also described by contemporaries as a wit, critic, and poet, although none of his verse was ever published, and above all a *bon viveur* who was not above the occasional debauch or wild escapade at court.

At the age of twelve, Nell's son was sent to be educated in France, learn French, and receive training in military administration, among other formal lessons, to prepare him for a life in the military and the court. When he was back in England, he enjoyed being with his father, especially at Newmarket. It was one place where his father used to go for a few days every spring and autumn, where he could enjoy 'putting off Majesty', mix freely among the crowd just like any country gentleman, and talk to the jockeys. With his parents' encouragement, young Burford would become a keen horseman early in life, an activity that he would enjoy for the rest of his years.

His little brother, James, Lord Beauclerk, showed no interest in such pursuits, and gave the court every impression of being something of a mother's boy. His health gave some cause for concern, he was evidently the weaker of the two, and his mother inevitably petted him a good deal more. Account books suggest that they suffered from constant coughs, colds, fevers, and stomach upsets, with regular purchases of syrup, plasters, cordial, and purging powder, as well as a cordial julep with pearls prescribed for Charles when he was four years old. At around the same age little James was quite ill, and bills show that he was regularly given an enema, three doses of purging powder, a cordial, and two ounces of discordium, a medicine made from dead leaves of water germander, which was prescribed for various complaints including fevers, digestive troubles, and insomnia.[30] Once he was considered strong enough, James was sent to school in Paris at the age of six, as it was generally accepted that education and deportment in the French capital were unrivalled anywhere else in Europe at the time.

In July 1679, Nell and Rose lost their mother, Helena. The press of the day did not hesitate to report that the middle-aged lady who had become an overweight alcoholic fell into a ditch, or into the River Thames, while she was drunk, and subsequently drowned. Her two daughters were the chief mourners at the funeral. James was in Paris and could not return for the occasion, while the king insisted that Charles should remain at Windsor with him, as he feared wild scenes on the streets.

Although only nine years old, the boy seemed more conscious of his royal inheritance, identifying himself with his father and slightly ashamed of his mother's humble origins as an actress of a 'poor' family and her past involvement with the oldest profession. That November, the king took the lad with him to Portsmouth to see a warship, named the *Burford* and launched in his honour, while Nell remained in London. Were there ever moments when the king might have wished that this son could change places with the maverick duke of Monmouth?

Little James died in Paris in June 1681. The circumstances of his life there and the cause of his death are unknown, one clue being that he died 'of a sore leg'. According to Beauclerk, this could have meant anything from an accident to poison.[31] Having lost her own mother the previous year, Nell was heartbroken at this second close bereavement within less than a year and went into deep mourning. As far as is known, she did not attend his funeral or visit his grave, and his place of burial remains a mystery.

*****

The only one of King Charles's significant mistresses who had not come from an English family was the Breton-born Louise Renée de Penancoët de Kéroualle, born on 5 September 1649. Her path from appointment as a maid to Queen Catherine to becoming one of the king's lovers was a brief one. Unlike the countess of Castlemaine, who never shrank from openly insulting the queen, Louise took care to show her all due respect. Queen Catherine had long since realised that what could not be cured in her husband must be endured, and relations between the French noblewoman and Portuguese-born queen consort would always remain civil, sometimes even almost friendly. The latter, who was not known for her love of anything French, was good at concealing her true feelings, disliked Louise intensely. While she had long accepted with reluctance that she must endure her husband's misdemeanours, she resented the fact that he should show more affection for a maid of honour than for his own wife.

The French ambassador, Charles Colbert, marquis de Croissy, could see the political advantage in a Frenchwoman becoming the king's mistress. In this he was aided by one of King Charles's favourite ministers, Secretary of State Henry Bennet, earl of Arlington, and his wife. Arlington was always keen to bring about a closer understanding between the courts of Britain and France. She had not long been a member of the royal household before it was noticed that the king evidently found her very attractive and good company. In October 1671, while he was at Newmarket for the races, he was invited by Arlington to stay at his nearby country estate, Euston Hall. Louise was there as well, and once Queen Catherine had returned to London on her own, the inevitable happened. John Evelyn recorded that events took their course:

> It was universally reported that the fair lady was bedded one of these nights, and the stocking flung after the manner of a married bride; I acknowledge that she was for the most part in her undress all day, and that there was fondness and toying with that young wanton … it was with confidence believed that she was first made *a Miss* [mistress], as they call these unhappy creatures, with solemnity at the time.[32]

Croissy was gratified that their plan had worked so well, and he reported with a sense of achievement to the marquis de Louvois, one of King Louis XIV's secretary of state for war and one of his favourite ministers, on their success:

> I have made Mlle de Kéroualle very joyful, by assuring her that his Majesty would be very pleased that she maintains herself in the good graces of the King. There is every appearance that she will possess them for a long time, to the exclusion of every one else.[33]

Louise was probably carrying his child by the time she and Charles returned to London. Charles Lennox was born on 29 July 1672, the youngest of the king's sons, and did not have to wait long to be ennobled. He was created 1st duke of Richmond, earl of March, and Baron Settrington in the Peerage of England on 9 August 1675 and duke of Lennox, earl of Darnley, and Baron Methuen of Torbolten in the Peerage of Scotland on 9 September 1675. He was invested as a Knight of the Garter on 18 April 1681, made governor of Dumbarton Castle three months later, and given the freedom of the borough in the town of Portsmouth. At the same time, his mother was officially appointed his tutrix and guardian, and he was granted an annuity of £2,000.

He also tried to secure the services of William Wycherley, best remembered for his licentious plays, as a tutor to his son. Wycherley had long been a much-favoured member of the inner court circle, enjoying the good conversation and also sometimes sharing the king's mistresses with him. Charles liked him, especially for his ready wit, and was sure that the dramatist would be well qualified to give the boy 'a princely education'. Believing there was more money in making a good marriage with a peer's daughter or a wealthy widow than with the hard work that tutoring a spoilt small boy would inevitably involve, he turned down the offer.

As the duke of Richmond reached adolescence, he was spending more time with his father, and gradually being introduced into official duties, as were his half-brothers who were living at Whitehall. Dinners were held by the mistresses for various ambassadors and foreign diplomatic visits, and these were often attended by some of the king's children. During the last year of the king's reign John Evelyn described him, and his half-brothers Northumberland and St Albans, accompanying Charles II for the Easter service at church. Richmond and St Albans, noted the diarist, were 'very pretty boys, and seem to have more wit than most of the rest'.[34]

*****

The support that Louise received from the French envoy was given on the understanding that she should serve the interests of her native sovereign. It remained a semi-formal undertaking, regularly confirmed by gifts and honours from Louis XIV, the most lavish being a pair of earrings worth £18,000, his most expensive gift to England that year and more lavish than any he had ever given Charles's queen. She remained obliged by loyalty to her sovereign in France to do what was expected of her.

Throughout her time in England, she was never well-liked. The contempt, bordering on hatred, openly avowed for her in the country was due as much to her own activity in the interest of France as to her promiscuity. Once when Nell, driving in a carriage through the streets of Oxford, was mistaken for her and surrounded by a potentially hostile crowd in Oxford in 1681, she announced unabashed, 'Pray good people be civil, I am the *Protestant* whore.' At once they realised their mistake and calmed down. In a relaxed age where monogamy and sexual morality were not regarded as essential, the term 'whore' (like that of 'bastard') was not the insult that it would become in a later age. Nell cared nothing for what the more prudish might think of her; in an age where Roman Catholics (or papists, as they were slightingly known) were viewed with suspicion, she was a lovable Protestant, a working-class girl who had done well for herself. In spite of her privileged position, she never pretended to have any airs or graces.

Louise looked down on Nell condescendingly as someone from the lower orders who had had to work for her living, referring to her as 'that pitiful strolling actress'.[35] Her withering comments were no match for the sharp wit of the former orange girl and actress, who could always answer back and leave the Frenchwoman on the back foot. One day, Louise told her: 'Why Nellie, you are grown rich, I believe, by your dress. Why woman, you are fine enough to be a queen!' 'You are entirely right, Madam,' Nell retorted, 'and I am whore enough to be a duchess.'[36]

It was inevitable that both women would be rivals, and not particularly friendly ones at that. They were totally dissimilar in background, Louise being a proud woman of noble birth used to the sophistication of the court at Versailles, while Nell was a high-spirited 'low-born' Londoner. Nell called the Frenchwoman 'Squintabella' as she had a cast in her eye, and the 'Weeping Willow' as she tended to burst into tears too readily. Sometimes they met for tea and cards, indicating that they were prepared to accept each other's presence after a fashion.

Yet Nell always resented Louise's superior attitude, the airs, graces, and pomposity that made her an easy target for teasing. Once when she felt unduly provoked, she tapped her on the shoulder and told her coldly that 'persons of one trade loved not one another'. It was also said that when the king asked Nell what he could do to appease parliament, she immediately replied, 'Hang the bitch.'[37]

The titles of Baroness Petersfield, countess of Fareham, and duchess of Portsmouth were granted to Louise for life on 19 August 1673. She could consider herself fortunate in more ways than one, for within a short space of time, her income in the form of allowances and pensions was considerable, to say nothing of regular gifts from the court at Paris. Yet a year later, she received another gift from the king, but a far less welcome one. With his free and easy not to say careless lifestyle, it was inevitable that sooner or later he would find himself on the receiving end of a sexually transmitted disease. In 1674, he was diagnosed with what was thought to have been syphilis, and he treated himself with mercury. It was too late from preventing him from infecting Louise, who became very ill and thereafter regularly suffered ill-health, even though she lived to a considerably greater age than any of the previous mistresses. Yet the indisposition was enough to prevent her from having a second child by him, and probably to ensure that they never shared a bed again.

Unlike the other ladies who had vied for the king's affections, or were still doing so, Louise was remarkably naïve. If his wandering eye was on the move, Barbara would be furious, then get even with him by carrying on an affair with some other beau. The more phlegmatic Nell, who knew that boys would be boys and men would be men, would shrug it off in the knowledge that he would soon come back to her. The ever-resigned Queen Catherine had long since accepted that he simply did not know the meaning of infidelity and it would not trouble him if he did. But when the duchess of Portsmouth found he had given her a very unpleasant contagious complaint, she took it to heart and stayed in her rooms for some time, refusing to see him. Deeply penitent, he sent her a magnificent pearl necklace and a large diamond, worth several thousand pounds. A French envoy, the marquis de Ruvigny, wrote to his colleague in France, the marquis de Pomponne, that both gifts had 'so rejoiced her that I should not wonder if, for the price, she were not willing to risk another attack of the disease.'[38]

Charles's conscience evidently troubled him, and this, coupled with her perception of his character, perhaps helps to explain how she retained her hold on him for the rest of his years. She escaped unscathed during the crisis of the Popish Plot in 1678, finding an unexpected ally in Queen Catherine, who initially resented her presence but appreciated the kindness and consideration Louise had always shown her. She maintained her position during a long illness in 1677 and in spite of a visit to France in 1682. One of Charles's nicknames for her was 'Fubbs', meaning plump or chubby. This female form was then much in vogue, and in 1682, the royal yacht HMY *Fubbs*, in reference to Louise's nickname, was built. If she was not flattered by this jocular reference to her generous girth, she kept her feelings to herself. In February 1685, she helped those at court to make sure that Charles II was received into the Catholic Church on his deathbed. Charles had been very attached to her, and one of his last instructions to his brother was to 'do well by Portsmouth', making her one of three women in his life, with the queen and Nell Gwynne, who were in his thoughts at the end.

Her privileged position allowed her to retain the apartments in Whitehall, which she kept for the rest of the reign. John Evelyn was present there at one of her levees in October 1683, but was evidently not impressed, writing caustically in his diary afterwards how glad he was as he 'went contentedly home, to my poor but quiet villa. Lord, what contentment can there be in the riches and splendour of this world, purchased with vice and dishonour?'[39]

4.

The son of Catherine Pegge, Charles Fitzcharles, or Charles Green as he became on his mother's marriage, had begun his education in the Netherlands and completed it in France, returning to London at the age of about fifteen. He and his father were more or less strangers, and one contemporary observed that King Charles 'hath not yet seen him, much less owned him'. Another, Sir Charles Lyttelton, a former governor-general of Jamaica, called him 'a fine youth ... they say he has a great deal of wit and is finely bred'.[40]

After getting to know the young man properly, the king was very impressed with him, felt he had a strong character, and felt suitably proud of having him in the family. Some at court felt it was possible that he was being viewed as a serious political rival to the duke of Monmouth, should there ever be any kind of struggle between them for the succession to the throne. In October 1672, Michael Boyle, archbishop of Dublin, noted a rumour that he was about to be given a commission as the colonel of the Queen's Regiment of Foot and granted an allowance of £10,000 *per annum*.

For a while, it looked as if this early promise was not to be fulfilled. He was allocated a pension of £2,000 a year from the excise, later increased to £4,000, but it threatened to be his undoing. Aware that he would never want for anything where finance was concerned, he moved into a suite of fashionable apartments at the Cockpit in the Palace of Whitehall, at the heart of the court and the governmental machine.

All this sudden paternal indulgence after early neglect had an unfortunate effect on his character and behaviour. He proceeded to run up debts without trying, especially with his tailor, and the sums would inevitably have to be settled by his father. A lover of fine decoration and furnishings, he indulged himself by hanging his rooms with the finest and most expensive damask, and he did not seem unduly concerned about paying his servants punctually. For want of anything else to do, he lay in bed almost every day until the afternoon. Plans were made to settle his liabilities if he promised that he would enrol at Cambridge University and dismiss the Roman Catholic servants, whom he had brought over from France and Flanders, but these came to nothing.

Lady Green feared that he must have fallen under disreputable influences and was far too easily led astray: 'much ill company [had] made him loose'. There was a lot of good in him, she believed, and it should not be allowed to go to waste. Somebody with strong leadership qualities needed to take charge of him, and he should be offered a thorough education. In 1674, King Charles appointed Sydney Lodge as his tutor and Robert Cheeke his governor, and for a while he proved himself a diligent student.

Towards the end of 1674, the extravagant, grossly spoilt, and perpetually debt-ridden young man and Lodge returned to the continent in the royal yacht *Portsmouth*, to spend some time studying in France. He was accompanied by Robert Paston, the younger brother of his brother-in-law Lord Paston. They were royally received by the governor of Calais, the duc de Charrost, and by all the other garrison towns through which they passed on their way to the south of France. Paston was soon able to write to Lady Green that her eldest son was benefiting from his experiences, greatly improving and above all pursuing his studies conscientiously with his reading the classical historians, such as Caesar, Sallust, and Aurelius Victor. He said that Mr Cheeke had recently written to the King, 'and did give a very good character of him, w[hi]ch I hope will make the King more kind to him'.[41] King Charles was evidently taking an interest in this son and doubtless hoped that great things could be expected of him in future.

In July 1675, he was created earl of Plymouth, Baron Dartmouth, and Viscount Totnes. As he had done with the duke of Monmouth, King Charles was anxious to select a suitable wife for him. By the summer of 1678, negotiations for his marriage to Lady Bridget Osborne, the daughter of the king's lord treasurer, the earl of Danby, were completed. On 19 September, they were married at Wimbledon Parish Church, with the groom taking the name of Charles Earle. Considering he had a responsibility to help his son-in-law something useful to occupy his time, Danby helped to secure a cornet's commission for him in a regiment serving in Flanders.

The prospect of army life appealed to his sense of adventure, but little was happening there. He became restless and hoped that his father could be persuaded to send him on campaign somewhere closer to the theatre of war, but nothing immediately came of this. Around this time, he became embroiled in an incident with the duke of Somerset which infuriated the king, probably connected with duelling, and probably impressed on him the necessity of keeping him out of mischief. The result was a role for him as a volunteer in the prince of Orange's army. On his return in 1679, he further tarnished his reputation by fighting a duel with Sir George Hewitt, his friend Charles, Lord Mordaunt, being his second. Neither man was injured, and they made it up afterwards, but such behaviour angered the king, who declared that he needed to be taught a firm lesson; they had to 'make him know he has no rank but what [I have] given him'.

Shortly afterwards, the king relented, feeling that the young man should have another chance to redeem himself. He allowed the earl to serve as a volunteer at Tangier, which had been acquired by England as part of the agreement when he married Catherine of Braganza. The marriage treaty was in effect a renewal of the long-standing Anglo-Portuguese alliance that had been signed in the fourteenth century. It was opposed by Spain, then at war with Portugal, but clandestinely supported by France. Like his predecessors for the last three centuries, King Charles was obliged to defend the interests of Britain's oldest ally Portugal and all its dominions to the utmost of his powers by sea and land. As a result, the English garrisoned and fortified the city against hostile but disunited Moroccan forces. The scheme did not meet with the unqualified approval of the government, which considered the territory was expensive to defend and fortify, especially as it constituted little commercial or military advantage to England.

In 1679, Moulay Ismail, sultan of Morocco, had made an unsuccessful attempt to seize Tangier, and imposed a strict blockade. Despite the drain on the public purse that it involved the city of Tangier, on the north coast of Morocco, which Portugal had included in Princess Catherine's marriage dowry, was strategically important for Britain as an overseas point of interest at the gate of the sea. It was also an important theatre of France's territorial and trading plans that threatened those of her neighbour Spain. Safeguarding British trade routes to the Levant and its lengthy coastline along the east of the Mediterranean from the ever-watchful Moorish and Algerian fleets to the south, required regular surveillance and also the possibilities of potentially lucrative trading centres.

In the summer of 1680, the earl of Plymouth was appointed as the founding colonel of the King's Own Royal Regiment as the 2nd Tangier, or Earl of Plymouth's Regiment of Foot. He welcomed the chance of going to serve his country, and had already left for the theatre of war, as had other recruits and the scratch force that had recruited members from the existing military establishment in England. His arrival in Tangier on 2 July served to bolster the morale of the other soldiers already serving at the garrison. He threw himself enthusiastically into drilling the troops, and he was charged with leading one of the columns that was ordered to attack the Moorish positions outside the city walls on 20 September.

Having taken the enemy by surprise, the British forces found it easy enough to occupy once more the entrenchments and outlying forts that they had abandoned to their enemies a long time before. The earl of Plymouth took his role seriously, ensuring that he was visibly part of the action and that the men under him knew he was in the thick of the operation. By the end of the day, the Moors had been repelled, and the victorious British contingent had begun building a stockade on the site of the Pole Fort, in order to anchor the centre of their position for future action.

At the beginning of the next month, Sir Palmes Fairborne, governor of Tangier, joined battle with the Moors who were besieging the port, and in its relief a squadron commanded by Rear-Admiral Sir John Berry was actively engaged. After all their hard work under a burning African sky, Plymouth was longing to quench his raging thirst. The water to which he had eagerly helped himself was contaminated, and he immediately fell ill with dysentery. Although he was taken back to the city to rest, he never recovered, and died of the 'bloody flux' on 17 October.

Some would say later that, for all his good qualities, he was an awkward, headstrong young man who could have caused problems for his father in later years. He might even have been tempted to make a bid for the crown, as did his half-brother the earl of Monmouth. Sending him out to serve on a campaign overseas from which he might not come back alive was, therefore, a prudent way to keep him occupied at a distance. It was persistently rumoured that he had been sent to sea in a leaking boat in order to get rid of him, but if that was the plan it did not succeed.

His servants brought their master's body home to England, but his high-spending youthful past would come back to haunt them. The estate was so deeply in debt that they were not allowed to land at Deal until a written promise was received from the Treasury, undertaking to pay the captain of the *Foresight* the money owed for their return passage. His body was therefore taken to London by Lord Mordaunt and laid to rest on 18 January 1681 in Henry VII's Chapel at Westminster Abbey, in a vault that had been left empty by the removal of the bodies of the Cromwell family. It was not only the end of him but also of the British presence in Tangier. Within a few years, they had blown up the harbour and defensive works they had been constructing and left the city, which was occupied and annexed by Moroccan forces. The earl of Plymouth and his wife left no children, and his titles became extinct.

*****

Barbara, countess of Castlemaine, had realised that her days of pre-eminence were now over. She saw that younger women at court were threatening her position and taking her place, and she no longer had the same hold on the king's affections. For too long, she had lived beyond her means. The king had given her plenty of money already, and refused to pay off the large gambling debts she was constantly running up. Desperately needing to economise, she had Nonesuch Palace demolished so the building materials could be sold off to meet them. In addition, she would need to leave England for a while and settle in Paris, where she could live more sparingly.

To prove she was a responsible mother, she decided to take her three youngest children, Henry, Charlotte, and George, and ensure they could be educated as she saw fit. The earl of Arlington strongly objected to the idea of Henry, his future son-in-law, being taken abroad. He wanted the boy to come and live with him at Euston, where he could be tutored privately and be trained as heir to the estates, but his mother stood firm: 'she will not part with him nor cares for any education other than what nature and her self can give him, which will be sufficient accomplishment for a married man'.[42]

George had inherited his father's swarthy looks as well as his height. On 1 October 1674, he was created baron of Pontefract, Viscount Falmouth, and duke of Northumberland. Once he, his mother, and siblings had settled, in the French capital, she found a tutor to come and give lessons to him and Henry, but both of them proved to be not reluctant students, but downright unruly. As George knew he was being prepared for life as the husband of the wealthy Lady Betty Percy, he knew that he could behave as badly as he liked and that his mother was unlikely to make much effort to try and control him. He refused to attend to his work, and persistently picked fights with the other boys. Before long, the despairing tutor had had enough, and he resigned his post.

Three years later, after the duke of Grafton had completed his education, she returned to England and tried to terminate the arrangement for the Arlington marriage. She thought the hand of Lady Percy, heir of the previous earl of Northumberland, would be more financially advantageous, but King Charles insisted that the original contract between the duke of Grafton, Isabella Bennet, and her family should be respected.

The wedding ceremony took place on 6 November 1679, and it was attended by John Evelyn among others. 'This sweetest, hopefullest, most beautiful child, and most virtuous too, was sacrificed to a boy that had been rudely bred', he noted, although he fervently hoped that she might have a good effect on the groom, and 'he may emerge a plain, useful and robust officer and, were he polished, a tolerable person for he is exceeding handsome, by far surpassing any of the King's other natural issue'.[43] On his marriage, he was given the additional titles of Baron Sudbury and Viscount Ipswich, and Charles II made him a Knight of the Garter on 30 September 1680. The following year, he was appointed colonel of the Grenadier Guards.

*****

On 11 August 1674, Anne, the eldest child of King Charles and the countess of Castlemaine, was married at Hampton Court to Thomas Lennard, 15th Baron Dacre, a gentleman of the bedchamber to the king, created earl of Sussex that same year. It is one of the few weddings of Charles II's children of which any description has survived:

> Dacre was brought at nine in the morning to the Duchess's apartments, and found the child-bride awaiting him there. A little after noon the King arrived from Windsor and led the procession from the Duchess's, through the Gallery, to the ante-camera of his own bedchamber. Charles walked first, holding the bride's hand; next came the bridegroom, next the Duke of York and the Duchess of Cleveland, and then Prince Rupert, followed by the ladies of the two contracting families. The ceremony was performed by the Bishop of Oxford, in the presence of those already named, together with the Duke of Monmouth, 'Don Carlos'—Charles's natural son by Catherine Peg, now Lady Green, who died five years later—the Earls of Suffolk, Arlington, Danby, and the Lord Keeper Finch. The service being over, the King kissed the bride, and 'by and by the

> bride-cake was broken over her head'—a proceeding which doubtless sounds more alarming than in reality it was. Finally there was a dinner in the Presence Chamber, at which the King had the bride on his right and her mother on his left. Soon after the wedding the little Countess was assigned rooms in Whitehall Palace, the same suite which had once been her mothers.[44]

A dowry of £20,000 from King Charles was promised as part of the marriage agreement, but much to the chagrin of the bride and groom, it was not paid for quite some time, if ever. Both of them were extravagant by nature, seemingly one of the few things they had in common. Ten years later, a scrutiny of the accounting books revealed that five different creditors were claiming almost £3,000 against the duchess of Cleveland for wedding dresses, 'gold and silver lace', and various other 'goods and chattels' supplied for the brides at both ceremonies. As usual, she had not paid the accounts, and King Charles was called upon to settle over half the debts. Within a few months, the king would be dead.

Matters were complicated when Ralph Montagu, English ambassador in Paris, who was successively the lover of both mother and daughter, the duchess of Cleveland and the countess of Sussex, befriended Hortense, Duchesse de Mazarin. A niece of Cardinal Mazarin, the late chief minister of France, she had become estranged from an abusive and mentally unstable husband. In her younger, more carefree days, she had been regarded as the perfect wife, not only for her beauty but also the dowry she would undoubtedly bring with her as a bride.

In 1659, the then-Prince Charles, who was more than a little smitten with her, had made enquiries for her hand but was rejected by her uncle, who regarded the British Commonwealth as a friendly power and had no wish to make an enemy of her, even if the prospects of the Stuarts at the time still looked uncertain. In January 1676, Montagu had brought her to court in London with the intention of making her the king's mistress in succession to the countess of Portsmouth. Tall, striking-looking, with a reputation for gambling, 'riding and drinking hard', shooting pistols, playing the guitar and dancing like a gypsy, to say nothing of a penchant for taking male and female lovers and cross-dressing, Hortense cut a colourful figure who had no intention of being ignored.

For a few months, she shared the king's bed, although this time there were to be no children. Louise was deeply upset at finding herself supplanted, taking to her bed again in her misery as she sobbed so much that others followed Nell Gwyn's lead in dubbing her the 'Weeping Willow'. Society was alternately scandalised and intrigued, not to say amused, when Hortense also embarked on a short-lived, but supposedly passionate relationship with Anne, countess of Sussex. It was said that not only had Hortense taught her to play shuttlecock and take part in Italian dances, but they were also spending their nights together, and even enjoying intimate relations with Mustapha, their oriental servant.

In July, at the age of fifteen, the countess had given birth to a daughter, whom she named Barbara after her mother. Lady Chaworth, a noted gossip of the age, wrote in great excitement of a public spectacle that was providing some unexpected entertainment. The countess and Madame Mazarin, she noted, had privately learnt to fence, 'and went down into St. James's Park the other day with drawn swords under their night gowns, which they drew out and made several fine passes with, to the admiration of several men that was lookers on in the Park'.[45] Whether they were clad in nothing but nightgowns, or more accurately evening coats, in a London park during what must have been a chilly December, is left to the imagination.

Even King Charles, with his notoriously relaxed moral outlook, was less than amused at the thought of his latest mistress and one of his daughters being involved in a lesbian relationship together and making such an exhibition of themselves, especially as the former, at thirty, was twice her age. As for the earl of Sussex, he was horrified. Lady Chaworth reported to her friends that husband and wife were certain to part 'unless she leave the Court and be content to live to [with] him in the country, he disliking her much converse with Madam Mazarine and the addresses she gets in that company'.[46] Anne also caused offence when she announced her plans to share a balcony in Cheapside with Hortense at the Lord Mayor's Show, prompting a stern letter from the countess of Castlemaine, lecturing her sternly on 'wifely obedience'.[47]

At length, the earl of Sussex warned his wife that it would be the end of their marriage unless she left the court at once and came to live in the country with him, far removed from such corrupting company. The king supported him, especially after Barbara had made her feelings of disapproval known as well. As she herself was known to have had a few same-sex dalliances herself, she was probably in no position to criticise her child for following in her footsteps—like mother, like daughter. Anne had no choice but to submit to pressure from all sides, crying bitterly as she was ordered away. She took to her bed, where she wept as she repeatedly kissed a miniature portrait of Hortense. By the end of January 1677, the family were so worried by her obsessive behaviour that they had to send for the doctors.[48]

Hortense, who was now dubbed 'the Italian whore' in England, had already received a pension from King Charles. More than satisfied with her mission presumably accomplished, she went back to Europe and found herself another male lover, Louis de Grimaldi, prince of Monaco. A furious King Charles, who did not take kindly to being made a fool of in this way, terminated her pension, but within a couple of days he had relented and agreed that he would continue the payments as promised. Nevertheless, it was the end of her time at the English court, and on the basis of 'better the devil you know', he returned to the arms of the duchess of Portsmouth.

The young Countess Anne soon got over the end of her sapphic dalliance with Hortense. She henceforth immersed herself in more respectable country activities such as hunting, hawking, and cricket, but this sedate existence soon palled for her. It is uncertain whether the earl handed her back to her mother, admitting that he simply could not manage her, or whether she walked out on him and decided to go back to the protection of her mother in France. While she was there, she became friends with Ralph Montagu and his wife, who both readily offered her their hospitality in Paris. Soon gossips were asserting that she was having an affair with Montagu, and that members of the French court, not known for their prudery, were horrified by her behaviour. Montagu's wife came instantly to her defence, saying that out of kindness they had invited her to come and stay because of her ill-health and depleted finances, and that to make any insinuations of propriety was a cruel slander.

In December 1677, Lady Chaworth wrote to her brother that the countess had put her daughter into a religious house, and 'she means certainly to come hither in the spring to either adjust things better between her and her lord, or get his consent that her daughter may go into orders'.[49] The countess of Castlemaine was furious. Although she was in no position to criticise anybody for profligacy, in a letter to King Charles she admitted that the earl of Sussex was a popular, though extravagant man, and thanks to his excessive spending and gambling losses, he had to sell Herstmonceux Castle and his estates.[50]

Meanwhile, the countess of Sussex had left her convent and seemed quite unashamed about openly flaunting her affair with Montagu. The king took the side of Barbara and recalled Montagu from Paris. Some said that the incorrigible ambassador returned to England before he could be dismissed from his post, but at any rate he was banished from court, struck off the Privy Council list, and all his requests for an audience with the king to defend himself were firmly refused. Several years later, after being restored to favour under James II, he became one of the first to give his wholehearted support to William, prince of Orange.

The wayward countess returned to England some four years later. She and the earl were reconciled, and they had three more children. Two sons, Charles and Henry, both died in infancy, but Anne, the youngest, lived to maturity, as did her sister, Barbara. The king readily forgave her for her scandalous behaviour, and they remained on the best of terms for the rest of his life. It appears, though, that she went her own way and openly continued to enjoy extramarital affairs.

Ever since Lucy Barlow's death in 1658, the belief had persisted that she and Prince Charles had gone through a form of marriage, that their son, James, duke of Monmouth, was legitimate, and that the king's childless marriage to Princess Catherine of Braganza in 1662 was bigamous. Foremost among them, not surprisingly, was the duke himself. Those who for one reason or another did not wish to see him become king saw it in their interests to blacken Lucy's name. Others looked on James, duke of York, as an uncompromising Catholic as opposed to his brother, a more liberal, easy-going one who kept his promise to respect liberty of conscience, a potential exponent of royalist absolutism like their father, and one who appeared too ready to accept the word of King Louis XIV and become utterly dependent on an over-mighty France at the expense of the British. They feared the prospect of him as their sovereign and thought the duke of Monmouth was much to be preferred as his father's successor. Only a legitimate heir would keep the duke of York off the throne.

The spectre would cast a long shadow over Lucy's erstwhile lover from the grave. In 1680, some two decades after she was laid to rest, King Charles made three separate official declarations that he was never married to her. James's succession to the throne depended upon the illegitimacy of Monmouth, so Lucy's reputation, it is said, had to be damned beyond redemption by James and his supporters to block any claim to the throne by her son. Her presence in British royal history remains a ghostly one. Had one or two events taken a slightly different course, she might have been a British queen consort, but all any biographer trying to piece together a chronological account of her short life will find is little more than a disordered collection of disputed accounts, if not a blank canvas. Was she a scarlet woman, an opportunist who only had to play her cards right and build support among a few influential champions to take her officially recognised place alongside King Charles II, and one who subsequently turned to blackmail when good fortune no longer shone on her? Or had they genuinely been husband and wife?

By around 1680, if not before, a sizeable faction in parliament seemed prepared to declare Monmouth legitimate by supporting the claim of his long-deceased mother that she and Charles II had indeed been married, albeit secretly. There was, they swore, a 'black box' in which Lucy had placed her marriage records and other documentary proof, and presented it for safe keeping to Anglican Bishop Cosin, whose death in 1671 left no direct witnesses to testify. Moreover, there had been a precedent in the case of King Edward IV's 'secret' marriage in 1464 to Elizabeth Woodville, although their eldest son, the twelve-year-old King Edward V, reigned for only a few weeks before being replaced by his uncle as King Richard III and never heard of again.

Over two centuries later, it was reported that in 1879 the Historical Manuscripts Commission came across an old black box among the 5th duke of Buccleuch's family papers at Dalkeith, and inside one of them was a legal contract of marriage between the couple. Assuming it was not a forgery, it could have provided proof that he was the rightful sovereign of Great Britain, a destiny for which he had absolutely no desire. On being shown the document, he threw it on to the fire, remarking that it 'might cause a lot of trouble'.[51]

The story was resurrected at the height of the Exclusion Crisis during the period from 1679 to 1681, when three exclusion bills sought to exclude the duke of York from the succession. This coincided with a thorough search for the black box. Witnesses came forward to swear that they had received the article from Cosin, or else that they had seen it in someone else's hands.

They were adamant that it contained a contract of marriage between the then-prince of Wales and Miss Lucy Walter, signed at a ceremony that had been performed by Dr William Fuller, bishop of Lincoln. In the meantime, the box and papers inside must have been lost or destroyed. Those who claimed to have seen its contents were summoned before the council and denied having seen any documents during the inquiry in 1680. Sir Gilbert Gerard, the son-in-law of Cosin, was summoned before the Privy Council. It was assumed that he either had the article in question, or else knew of its whereabouts. He denied any knowledge of where it was, in spite of his earlier allegations that his father-in-law left it to him and that he had found the marriage contract.

King Charles also stated emphatically that no marriage between Lucy Walter (or Barlow) had ever taken place, and he swore on oath to the Privy Council three times in this period and twice for publication in the government newspaper that in his whole life he had only once been through a ceremony of marriage once, his bride being Queen Catherine. One witness was found to testify that Margaret Sambourne, an aunt of Lucy Barlow, had told her that she was legally married to the king. Another said that he knew of a bishop who could not only attest to having performed the marriage ceremony but could also produce the names of the witnesses who had attended. Yet another declared that Oliver Cromwell's officers had confiscated the marriage certificate from Lucy Barlow while she was under arrest. Others were sure that all birth and wedding records in Lucy's home county of Pembrokeshire in the year of Monmouth's birth were destroyed at the Restoration.

King Charles always loved his eldest son, giving him every civil or military honour it was in his power to bestow. Yet he could not give Monmouth the prize he most coveted: that of legitimacy and therefore the likelihood, almost certainty, of a throne on his death. His whole life was overshadowed by his bastardy, and the inescapable knowledge that his mother had almost certainly been a whore. One point of view suggests that this was not regarded by all as a major sin, for Nell Gwyn cheerfully called herself 'the Protestant whore' and was much loved in Restoration England, Monmouth, but the would-be heir to the throne, felt it deeply. Only a century and a half later, the Fitzclarences, the ten illegitimate children of William, duke of Clarence and later King William IV, by actress Dorothea Jordan, never ceased to curse what they called their 'very peculiar position'. It was a cross that the eldest, George, earl of Munster, carried throughout a life dogged in his final years by depression, ending in an early death by his own hand.

The country at large saw how much the monarch loved his son, but were not to know anything of the private side of their sometimes stormy relationship. Monmouth was a headstrong young man, used to getting his own way. Vain, susceptible to flattery and manipulation, he was not afraid to try and cultivate senior ministers of the time if necessary. He also had one great advantage, namely a valuable ally close to his father in Nell Gwyn. She liked and readily sympathised with the young man, and was always ready to put in a good word for him if it was needed. They remained on the best of terms until his death, and knew they could always speak their minds to each other, sometimes with harsh words but never lasting resentment. He could confide in her as he could in nobody else, except perhaps his wife, while she appreciated his support and looked on him as one of her truest friends in a court that had initially viewed her with suspicion.

Although she was a few months younger than him, he regarded her as a mother figure, in view of the sometimes-dissolute parent whom he remembered but little. His childhood had been dominated at irregular intervals by her, and his father had often tried to remove him from her care. Nell could readily understand his feelings as an outsider, while she always took care to remember that it was in his best interests that his aspirations to wearing the crown after his father was dead should be gently discouraged. Sometimes it was not the advice he wanted to hear from her. After one acrimonious exchange between them, he angrily called her a guttersnipe, at which she snapped back, 'Was Mrs Barlow better bred than I?'[52]

For most of King Charles II's reign, Monmouth had enjoyed a good relationship with his uncle. The duke of York was impressed with his nephew's bravery under fire in battle, and his leadership skills, and they sometimes went hunting together. On one occasion in 1673 when they dined together, it was noticed by others that the elder man seemed very proud of his nephew's success, and that he evidently had 'a particular kindness and affection' for him. Yet when it became evident that the younger man was beginning to see himself as a king-in-waiting, he allowed himself to be encouraged by some of those around him as such, even to the point of allowing his health to be drunk as prince of Wales.

Yet by this time, their relationship was about to corrode, with the gradual ending of Monmouth's years of good behaviour and caution.

It was probably inevitable that one day their patience with each other would snap. Ever since the Restoration, there had been a sense among sections of parliament and also Protestant opinion in the country at large that the king's relationship with an over-mighty France under King Louis XIV and other Catholic rulers of Europe was too close for comfort. Roman Catholicism was synonymous with absolute rule, and while King Charles was publicly Anglican, he and his brother's Catholic sympathies were no secret. Such suspicions hardened especially after it was confirmed in 1673 that the duke of York had become a Roman Catholic. The king was known for his tolerance of other religions, while his brother was seen as being the exact opposite.

It led to an unsettled period, culminating in the Popish Plot, a fabricated conspiracy created by the disgraced priest Titus Oates. In 1678, he warned King Charles that a group of Catholics was planning to assassinate him. During the accusations and charges that followed, and the subsequent anti-Catholic hysteria, at least twenty innocent men, probably many more, were found guilty and executed on fabricated evidence. The charade only came to an end when Oates overreached himself and, in an act of remarkable folly, informed the king that Queen Catherine was involved in an attempt to poison him. He was arrested and imprisoned, released but later arrested on a charge of sedition, heavily fined, and imprisoned.

*****

Though the duke of York was regarded by King Charles as his successor, with Monmouth having other ideas, one of the king's other sons was seen as having a possible claim on the crown, although it was an extremely weak one that few people ever took seriously.

The duchess of Portsmouth knew how weak her position was in England. It has been suggested by one of her recent biographers that as a girl, she had dreamed of becoming queen of England.[53] The 1st earl of Shaftesbury was an experienced parliamentarian since the reign of Charles I and now lord president of the council. As a fervent Anglican, like many others who shared his beliefs, he saw Roman Catholicism as tantamount to arbitrary government, and the prospect of a committed Catholic on the throne in a few years' time as a major threat to the rule of parliament. As suspicion of his commitment to Catholicism grew and his popularity throughout England fell, Shaftesbury encouraged Louise to believe that the duke of York could probably be excluded from the succession, and King Charles could therefore nominate his heir. Although the exclusion of illegitimate issue would be debarred, making his elder niece, Mary, princess of Orange, next in line, it would therefore be quite feasible for him to choose the young duke of Richmond, who resembled him so much, the son of his favourite mistress. He had been brought up a Protestant, and being half-French, as king would find a powerful ally in King Louis XIV.

What Monmouth might have thought of such a scenario evidently did not cross their minds. Yet Louise, who evidently did not know that King Charles took the order of succession to the throne seriously and was not likely to be persuaded to dismiss it so lightly, seemed to find the scheme quite feasible. Quite why Shaftesbury, who was already known as a supporter of Monmouth's claim, should have allowed to convince herself that it might have been possible is hard to explain. Maybe he believed that she could somehow use her powers over her besotted lover and sovereign to get what she wanted. If the duke of York became too unpopular, it was possible to believe that if he did ascend the throne, he could lose it again very quickly, especially if a stronger candidate could lay claim. Yet the young and untested duke of Richmond, illegitimate son of a much-disliked foreign mistress, was certainly not that person. King Charles was not ready to exclude his brother from the succession; on the contrary, future events would show how hard he fought to retain as his heir a brother whom he did not particularly like. If he was not going to be persuaded to name his eldest son, Monmouth, as heir, he was certainly not likely to hand such a coveted price to a much younger one.

Ironically, it was at about this time that Monmouth was about to prove his worth to everyone in what was arguably the most successful point of his career. After the Restoration, the Presbyterians were finding themselves increasingly persecuted for their beliefs, and a small armed rising had been put down in 1666. Some of them took the law into their own hands and held illegal outdoor meetings, known as conventicles. They were often broken up by government forces, notably those led by John Graham of Claverhouse, who had been put in charge of putting down many of these assemblies. On 1 June 1679, he encountered one at Loudoun Hill, but his troops were routed by armed Covenanters at the Battle of Drumclog, and he fled to Glasgow. After this victory, the Covenanters spent the next few weeks building their strength, as did the government.

King Charles nominated Monmouth captain-general of his forces and sent him north to put down the rebellion. At another battle, fought nearby at Bothwell Bridge, the numerically superior Covenanters were quickly routed, with losses of about 800 men, Monmouth appreciated the virtues of magnanimity in victory, to say nothing of pursuing a mission to reduce bitterness and tension in Scotland. When he found that his men were executing the vanquished prisoners they had taken, he ordered them to cease forthwith, and on his orders, around 1,200 survivors were to be treated with dignity, and taken to Edinburgh where his own surgeons could dress their wounds.

He returned south to be acclaimed as a hero by some, but a threat by others in attempting to court popularity with the masses any way he could. He went to make a report to the council at Hampton Court, and then to Windsor to be received by the king. At first, he congratulated his son, but when told about the aftermath of the battle, he said that 'if he had been there they should not have had the trouble of prisoners'. Monmouth humanely answered that he 'could not kill men in cold blood; that was only for butchers'.[54]

In August, King Charles fell ill with a fever. His condition gave increasing concern for several days, provoking much concern among ministers as to what would happen if he was to die. Because of the state of alarm and general disquiet created by the Popish Plot, the presence of the duke of York was regarded as mildly inflammatory, and in March 1679, King Charles had asked him to leave England for what amounted to a kind of voluntary exile, in Brussels.

The earl of Shaftesbury, a fervent supporter of Monmouth, was determined to keep the duke of York from returning. Meanwhile, the duke of York's supporters, and probably the duke as well as the king, were sure that Shaftesbury was encouraging Monmouth in setting his sights on the throne, and also in trying to convince him that the Catholic heir had an 'irreconcilable hatred of his person', which they felt was untrue.[55] The duke of York may not have trusted his nephew, or those around him who were plainly a bad influence, but at this stage does not seem to have harboured feelings of hatred towards him.

Monmouth had his own reasons for suspicion, for York, although both wives had given him legitimate children, also had several by various mistresses, and also seemed over-friendly with the duchess of Monmouth. Like his father, the duke was never a shining example of fidelity to the woman he had married, but he did not take kindly to her being too friendly with his uncle. Whether it was because of their personal over-familiarity, or whether he thought the duke of York was trying to make an obedient Catholic out of her, is uncertain.

There was no clear solution to what might happen. If Monmouth could not succeed as king, because of the taint of illegitimacy, might he become another protector like Oliver Cromwell before him, pledging himself to safeguarding the liberties of the people with the right, like-minded political allies ready to support him, or would he put himself at the head of a constitutional monarchy? Another school of thought was neither pro-York nor pro-Monmouth. Its adherents wanted to save the country from the prospect of a second civil war within forty years, and they thought there could be a solution in calling on the Protestant Mary, princess of Orange, as second in succession after her father, the duke of York, to act as a more acceptable regent for her father. They secretly sent a message to him, asking him to come home as soon as possible. Much to Monmouth's annoyance, he arrived at Windsor on 2 September. Some ministers fared that the Protestants might take the law into their own hands, with anti-papist mobs and demonstrators seizing control of London and the cities and turning on the Roman Catholics.

Fortunately, there were no disturbances, and the king recovered a few days later. As a result, there was no need for the duke of York to stay in England any longer, and it was suggested to him that he could return. The king also feared that if his brother stayed in England, he could be a threat to the monarchy. He asked permission to go to Scotland instead of Brussels, where he would need to go to collect the duchess of York and then move back to the British mainland. He also made his departure conditional on the duke of Monmouth being sent away as well. His requests were accordingly granted.

A few days later, King Charles dismissed Shaftesbury from the post of lord president of the council. Monmouth was deprived of his rank of lieutenant-general, temporarily banished from all three kingdoms, and ordered abroad again. Though the king did not make his reasons public, he was angry with his son for his open opposition to the duke of York, for his reckless association with opposition leaders in the City of London, and because of his unashamed courting of popularity in England and in Scotland, which was almost tantamount to setting up his own rival court. Monmouth went to The Hague and was again welcomed by William of Orange with such lavish hospitality that the duke of York found it necessary to remonstrate with him.

He was also offered a command in the Polish army which he was tempted to accept. However, he still felt that his position as possible heir to the British throne would prevent him from doing so. It was suspected that he and various friends or sympathisers might be actively searching for witnesses prepared to swear that King Charles was married to Lucy Barlow, and any documents still in existence that might be taken as proof of the marriage. At the end of November, without permission from his father, he returned to London, sending his father a message that he wished to prove his innocence of any connection with the recent Popish Plot, such as it was.

Nell Gwyn had always remained a good and loyal friend to him, always ready to give him the benefit of her advice while not being afraid to tell him when she thought he might be acting foolishly. He tried to use her as an intermediary in order to arrange an interview with his father and plead his innocence. When he approached her, she told him she felt he was acting unwisely by giving the impression that he was appearing to set himself up as a prince of Wales in all but name, even to the extent of mocking his pretensions and calling him 'Prince Perkin', a teasing reference to Perkin Warbeck, the unsuccessful pretender in Henry VII's reign who had ended his life on the scaffold at Tyburn.

Although she was critical of his behaviour and thought it only fair to tell him so, she was touched and saddened by the unhappiness he evidently felt in being estranged from his father. If anybody could build a bridge between them, she knew, the one person in a position to do so was her. She begged the king to receive him and hear his side of the story, but he refused and ordered her to be quiet. The fact that his son was staying with her at her house was apparently kept from him, as they both feared the extent of his anger if he should find out, but he knew that they were keeping closely in touch. When Monmouth insisted that he was going to stay in England and pursue the matter of exclusion of the duke of York in defiance of the king's orders, Nell realised that he had gone too far.[56] Much as she liked him, she had no alternative but to order him out of her house, albeit with a heavy heart. Her first loyalty was to his majesty, and she could not possibly give sanctuary to a rebel whose actions were verging on treason to the crown. He complied with her wishes but refused to go abroad.

One reason why he insisted on staying in London as long as possible was the sudden illness of his youngest son. Two-year-old Francis was ailing and died on 4 December, a week after his father's arrival in London. King Charles sent one of his half-brothers, the duke of Grafton, to go and offer his condolences in person to the grieving duchess, but he was instructed not to say a word to her husband. By this time, the duke and duchess had drifted apart. Although their marriage did not end in divorce, it was clear to all that they were estranged, and their union was effectively over. The duke was now spending more time with his mistress, Eleanor Needham, who gave him a son and two daughters.

Had the Exclusion Bills, or rather the bill that was presented three times in the House of Commons, been passed, it would have paved the way for the duke of Monmouth, regarded as the great hope of the British Anglicans, to become heir and succeed his father as king. Much as he loved his son, the king continued to prove unfailingly loyal to his brother. He put an end to the matter by using his royal prerogative to dissolve parliament, on three separate occasions between 1679 and 1681, leaving his opponents with no lawful method of preventing the duke of York's succession.

Monmouth was anxious to show himself to the people and cement his status as the great Protestant hope. With the ready encouragement of Shaftesbury, in order to boost his following in the provinces, he made two progresses. The first began in 1680 in Chichester and continued through Dorset, Somerset, and Devon. He received an enthusiastic reception wherever he went, and as he entered on Bath, a crowd of 200 citizens on horseback greeted him to escort him to the city centre, where bonfires had been lit and bells were pealing.

Such a display infuriated his father, who was fast losing patience with him, and told Sir Leoline Jenkins, one of his ministers, he disliked what he was doing so much that he 'desires his friends not to show him any respect nor to have any commerce with him in this ramble'.[57] Yet he met with no noticeable opposition on his travels. One episode that went down very well with the community was while he was staying at Ilchester and met Elizabeth Parcet, a girl suffering from scrofula, or 'the King's Evil'. She came forward and touched his hand, and her recovery within forty-eight hours was all they needed to place their faith in him as the rightful heir.

A similar progress further north two years later in Cheshire and Staffordshire saw him similarly greeted with enthusiasm, although a group of court supporters at Lichfield hired a room to his own, shouted him down and drank to the health of the duke of York. Yet King Charles was deeply angered by his son's shameless courting of adulation, behaving as if he was already heir to the throne. While Monmouth was walking along the streets of Stafford on 20 September, he was arrested, charged with disturbing the public peace, and taken back to London. The king refused to receive him and forbade him to appear at court. Later he stripped his son of his position of as master of the horse and replaced him with his young stepbrother, the duke of Richmond. Being only ten years old at the time, the boy was not expected to undertake any of the corresponding duties himself, and two commissioners were appointed to carry out necessary work.

That autumn there were rumours of a conspiracy, even a *coup d'état*, masterminded by some of the more republican elements. Whispers abounded of establishing a republic another Commonwealth, perhaps with Monmouth as lord protector, or as Stadtholder on the same basis as in the Netherlands. Realising that he was losing control of the situation and that the assassination, or even capture, of his father was the last thing he would countenance, he saw that now was the time for behaving with greater circumspection. Lord Shaftesbury, who was regarded as the ringleader of the conspirators and fearing that he was about to be arrested, disguised himself as a priest and fled to Holland. Old and ill, he died a few weeks later. A series of risings planned for 18 November was halted.

Yet there was to be no peace for King Charles, his brother, or his son. Early in 1683, a further conspiracy was formulated but never came to fruition. The Rye House Plot, centred on Rye House near Hoddesdon, Hertfordshire, was devised with the objective of assassinating the king and the duke of York as they returned from a visit to the races at Newmarket races to London at the beginning of April. A major fire at the town resulted in cancellation of the races, and the conspirators found their plans frustrated by the brothers' enforced change of plan.

It was soon established that there were two separate plots. One, led by a veteran officer who had served under Oliver Cromwell, aimed to kill the king and the duke of York, while another, involving Monmouth and various aristocratic figures, stopped short of assassination but proposed to occupy Whitehall, call the nation to arms, and establish a republic under the leadership of Monmouth. Everyone who knew him well could attest that he was too susceptible to flattery and persuasion, always liable to be swayed by stronger characters and in danger of being talked into extreme courses of action in which he never felt comfortable. One of his less dependable allies was Robert Ferguson, a Scottish Presbyterian minister renowned for his treasonable schemes, and known as 'the Plotter'. He was an ardent supporter of Monmouth's claim to the throne against that of the duke of York, and during the ensuing years he proved remarkably adept at escaping from England and eluding capture far more effectively than most of his peers, who were left to face and often suffer for the consequences.

On 18 June, the Privy Council issued a proclamation for apprehending Monmouth, Ferguson, and others for 'treasonable consultations to levy Men and make an Insurrection in our Kingdom'. It was altered a day later to accuse the named persons of planning 'the Death and Destruction of Our Royal Person and of Our Dearest Brother', and offering a reward of £500 for the capture of each. Monmouth laid low by going quietly to the house of his new mistress Henrietta Wentworth, at Toddington, Berkshire, where he remained in hiding. Her home, unlike that of his previous amour, Eleanor Needham, was not under surveillance.

Although he might be a thorn in his father's side, he stopped short of desiring his father's death, let alone lift a finger to assist anybody with this objective. He told the king to his face that 'there is nothing [that] has struck me so to the heart as to be put into a proclamation for an intention of murdering you.'[58] The duchess of Monmouth was equally mortified, as she knew that she would be severely tainted by association and that it would risk her family forfeiting their estates and titles. Although she and her husband were by now largely estranged, she was expecting another child, and she gave birth prematurely to a tiny stillborn daughter, Charlotte.

While it is easy to accept that Monmouth would never have knowingly been party to assassinating his father or uncle, his behaviour over the previous few years had been increasingly foolish, and his enemies cold have been forgiven for doubting his innocent assurances. While his guilt was never proved, it was evident that he had had close contact with some of the conspirators. One of those implicated, the earl of Essex, was imprisoned in the Tower of London and cut his throat while awaiting trial, while several others were either executed, imprisoned, or exiled.

It was becoming increasingly difficult for the king to trust him at all. He was now living with his mistress, Henrietta Wentworth, and he was allowed to remain in hiding, thanks to his father's readiness to forgive. Nevertheless, at a subsequent interview between both, his penitence did not appear more than skin deep. With a heavy heart, his father ordered him back to Holland on what amounted to banishment. He promptly found a warm welcome from his cousins William and Mary, prince and princess of Orange. William had not emerged totally unscathed from the Rye House controversy, as some of the conspirators had escaped to Holland in order to avoid trial.

6.

As John Evelyn had foreseen at the time of his marriage in 1679, the duke of Grafton's future lay as an officer, and the king had decided he was going to enter the navy. In 1678, he had served in the Mediterranean aboard the frigate HMS *Happy Return* under Captain Sir William Poole, a senior officer who had fought in the Anglo-Dutch wars. In January 1680, he was entrusted to veteran officer Sir John Berry and returned to the Mediterranean in the frigate HMS *Leopard*. During the next few months, he visited Alicante and Malaga on the Spanish coast, and also Tangier, where his half-brother, the earl of Plymouth, also saw active service but from which he never returned alive. Grafton was more fortunate.

This expedition was his first chance to demonstrate his courage in battle as well as his knowledge of naval warfare. His experience of the army and navy would ensure he had the finest qualities of both. His potential as an officer was recognised by the king and also by those who worked with him, and he was acquiring a reputation as one of the most able of Charles II's sons. As Monmouth had previously served with some distinction but latterly disgraced himself in the eyes of many, his half-brother looked set to take over his mantle as a more dependable asset to the kingdom's armed forces.

Leaving the ship, he returned to England at the end of the year. From that time onwards, he was well rewarded with offices and promotion. He was made colonel of the 1st Foot Guards in 1681 and served as master of Trinity House in 1682–3. On 13 January 1683, he became vice-admiral of England in succession to Prince Rupert, the king's cousin who had died the previous year. Three months later, on 24 April, he was appointed admiral and commander-in-chief in the narrow seas and took command in July of the new third-rate named HMS *Grafton* in his honour, a vessel of seventy guns that he had fitted out at his own expense.

To the annoyance of Grafton and his mother, he was suddenly recalled at the end of the month. In his place, George Legge, Baron Dartmouth, sailed at the head of the fleet to Tangier with instructions to evacuate the colony, a task that otherwise might have been entrusted to him. Dartmouth, a veteran commander from the Anglo-Dutch wars, was the choice preferred to the younger man on account of his seniority and previous experience.

Later in the year, he was in command of his own squadron. By order of the lords of the admiralty (Viscount Brouncker, the first president of the Royal Society, Sir Edward Hales, and Henry Savile), the duke of Grafton, admiral of the Narrow Seas, was to hold a court-martial to try some mutineers on board the *Bonaventure* and also the boatswain of the *Mary Rose*, who was charged with killing a man. A letter from an unknown to Lord Preston suggested that Dartmouth was not going as had been planned, it was announced that the duke of Grafton had returned from the Downs, 'and it appears from the number of ships and provisions on board that he goes to Tangier at least, and not to survey the western coast and the isles of Jersey and Guernsey, as was given out'.[59]

There would be further good news to follow in the autumn. During the previous year, the duchess, aged fourteen, had been expecting a child which she lost early in her pregnancy. The earl of Arlington wrote to the duke of Ormond, lord lieutenant of Ireland in October 1682 to express his concern at the state of her well-being: 'I cannot omit telling you what an alarm we were under last week by my Lady Grafton's miscarriage, which, tho' it proved so, yet she is now, God be thanked, in good health.'[60] One year later, on 23 October 1683, she gave birth to a son, and the family were overjoyed. In a contemporary letter, an anonymous friend said the maternal grandfather was so happy that he wanted to 'smother it with kisses'. The new arrival was named Charles after the king.

John Evelyn noted in his diary:

> I went to compliment the Duchess of Grafton, now laying in of her first child, a son, which she called for, that I might see it. She has become more beautiful, if it was possible, than before, and full of virtue and sweetness. She discoursed with me of many particulars, with great prudence and gravity beyond her years.[61]

In April 1684, Grafton went to France and met Louis XIV, who was suitably impressed with his abilities and realised he could be useful if required.

As a result, he was briefly employed at the siege of Luxembourg during the war between France and Spain that summer, and then came back to Paris in 26 July to return home. That same year, he received a warrant to succeed Sir Robert Holmes as governor of the Isle of Wight, when the latter was charged with misconduct, but before he could take up his duties Holmes was acquitted by court-martial and retained his post.

Knowing that this promising son was keen for further adventure and military experience, King Charles intended to keep the duke of Grafton gainfully employed. Increasingly disappointed in Monmouth's behaviour with his obsession to promote himself as the rightful heir to the throne instead of the duke of York, Charles's main hopes were pinned on Grafton. He therefore decided to send him to the French court at Condé. As a result, he was briefly employed at the siege of Luxembourg during the war between France and Spain that summer. Situated between the kingdom of France and the Habsburg territories to the east, the city and fortress of Luxembourg was of considerable strategic importance. Under Spanish control at the start of 1684, it was regarded as a vital prize by France, and during a six-week siege lasting from April to June that year, it was captured by France, although with considerable casualties on both sides. A truce followed and Grafton returned to England at the end of July, taking with him the gift from a grateful King Louis XIV of a sword set with diamonds.

*****

While the duke of Northumberland was growing up, his father was keen that he should see something of the world, and he spent some time travelling throughout Europe. During adolescence he visited Venice, the Netherlands, and Luxembourg. Wanting to experience military service again, he served as a volunteer alongside the French army at Courtrai and, like the duke of Grafton, at the siege of Luxembourg in summer 1684, returning to England in the autumn. John Evelyn, who met him at dinner at Sir Stephen Fox's in October, soon after his return, was quite fulsome in his praise:

> He seemed to be a young gentleman of good capacity, well-bred, civil and modest.... Of all his Majesty's children (of which he has now six Dukes) this seemed the most accomplished and worth the owning. He is extraordinarily handsome and-well shaped.[62]

Charles Beauclerk had spent another couple of years being educated in France, and he returned to England on what was supposed to be a short visit over Christmas in the closing weeks of 1683. However, after the death of Henry Jermyn, 1st earl of St Albans, on 5 January 1684, King Charles decided to grant his son the title of duke of St Albans. He also gave him an allowance of £1,000 a year and granted him the offices of chief ranger of Enfield Chace and master of the hawks in reversion (after the death of the current incumbents). He moved into apartments in the palace that he shared with his half-brothers and began his life as a courtier. If the duke of Monmouth had proved a major disappointment to the king, then maybe this half-brother's promise would be some consolation to him in his last years.

*****

In 1683, King Charles told Paul de Barrillon, appointed French ambassador to the English court six years earlier, that the duchess of Portsmouth and the duke of Richmond were the two people for whom he had 'the utmost affection'. He would be most grateful, he said, if the king of France would consent to raise the estate of Aubigny to a duchy for her and, after her decease, for him as well.[63] Barrillon had long been annoyed by the king regularly making such demands and wrote to King Louis on the matter, adding a complaint regarding the demands being made by or on behalf of 'the favourite', but the latter made no objection. In December 1683, he conferred upon her the title duchess of Aubigny in the Peerage of France, with the proviso that Richmond would inherit the dukedom on her death.

The king enjoyed having his young sons with him, and had high hopes that when they were adults, they would be able to play suitable supporting roles in the country, whether in the armed forces, the church, or any other walk of life. Known as 'the fraternity', the half-brothers had rooms at Whitehall Palace. Evelyn recorded on his diary on 30 March 1684, Easter Day, that he attended the service at Whitehall where the bishop of Rochester preached to his majesty, and three of his sons, the dukes of Northumberland, Richmond, and St Albans, were also in the congregation.

At various times in his life, King Charles was devoted to each of his children. However, in his last years, the ever-unpredictable Monmouth sorely tried his patience, and he sometimes must have wondered if and when he and his eldest son should meet again. Ever the optimist, Monmouth never gave up on his ultimate ambition. In the autumn of 1684, he paid a private visit to England, accompanied by Henrietta Wentworth, and on 30 November, he had a secret interview with his father. He had been warned that the duke of York and what he called 'his Jesuitical cabal' were actively conspiring 'how to take the King off the stage'. The duke of York, whose intelligence services were well primed to watch out for such comings and goings, was aware of his presence in England, but assumed that his nephew was on a mission to secure his mistress's estates. He thought that Monmouth had exhausted the king's remarkable fund of goodwill, and he doubted if there was any chance of a reconciliation between them.

On his arrival in London, Monmouth arranged a meeting with Lord Alington, constable of the Tower of London and a trusted friend, to acquaint him with the facts as well. Whether Monmouth actually had a meeting with his father on this visit or not is open to doubt, but most historians suggest that they probably did not come face to face, inferring that Alington was the one who regularly passed the news on to his majesty about the duke of York's nefarious plans.

Whatever the truth of the matter, the king sent for Alington and asked what he thought he should do. The constable told him sadly that he had brought the situation upon himself by turning the duke of Monmouth out, and 'suffering such to be put in who are the Duke of York's creatures'. His advice, he said, was to order the duke of York to go to Scotland, to hold the next session of his parliament as he was due to do. Once he arrived, his majesty should 'send for the Duke of Monmouth, restore him to all his places, and remove from the Court all persons that are suspected to favour the Duke of York's interest'.[64] Spies, presumably in the employ of the duke of York and his supporters, were listening behind the curtain, and lost no time in passing on the supposedly confidential information.

The king's probable motives, or at least his most satisfactory solution to what must have seemed like an insoluble problem that was beyond his control, are perhaps best explained by the contemporary historian James Welwood, who wrote about fifteen years later:

> King Charles, tired out at last with the uncontrolled hardships that were every day put upon him by the Duke [of York]'s creatures, and ashamed to see his own lustre obscured, and his Power lessened by a party that had raised themselves upon Monmouth's Ruin, he resolved to shift the Scene; and in order to make himself easy for the rest of his life, as he

> expressed it, he determined to send away the Duke of York and recall Monmouth.
>
> April was the time agreed to put on to this resolution in practice; but there is little left us by which we can judge whether Monmouth was to be recalled to court by a formal invitation of the King's, or whether King Charles's usual thread of dissimulation was to be spun out to that length that Monmouth was to land with an armed force. The first seems more probable, if it were but for what he has writ himself in the Pocket-book.... It's true, the last looks more of a piece with the rest of his Behaviour towards his brother and son, and more agreeable to his natural bias, which seldom inclined him to choose the high road, when there could possibly be found a by-path to tread in.[65]

Welwood was certain that King Charles had absolutely no intention of altering the line of succession in Monmouth's favour, or to do anything that might make it easier for him to seize the crown after he had died. His main objective was more probably to weaken the power of the duke of York's supporters by slightly strengthening those of Monmouth's party as a counterbalance if possible. This, opined George Roberts, one of Monmouth's earliest biographers, was perfectly consistent 'with the only fixed maxims of government in that reign, that when any one party grew too strong, to throw in the royal weight into the lightest scale'.[66]

Later that month, as Alington had advised, King Charles told the duke of York that he would have to go to Scotland to preside over the Scottish session in February. York had been well prepared for this. Moreover, in view of the delicate situation that seemed to be involving both brothers and the semi-exiled illegitimate son, he was immediately suspicious that any such mission that would require his absence some distance away from London would be tantamount to banishment for him as well. He refused, saying that he had pressing business reasons for staying in London. The king told him quietly that he would have to go, 'or I must go.' Despite York's obstinacy, King Charles made his wishes clear in his presence before the council, saying that his royal highness was going to proceed to Edinburgh in February.

Monmouth was kept regularly informed on such arrangements, receiving letters from King Charles to stay in Holland until advised of any further developments, and from the marquis of Halifax to trust in his cousin William of Orange, would 'certainly have leave to return' to

England in February. Halifax had long been one of Monmouth's most trusted supporters and one of the standard-bearers of the Protestant cause in parliament.

*****

For some time, King Charles II had been increasingly troubled by gout. He had always been fond of walking his spaniels in St James's Park, but by now he was finding even gentle exercise increasingly difficult. On 1 February 1685, he complained of pain in his leg, saying he did not feel well, but was sure it would soon pass. In the evening, he went to visit the duchess of Portsmouth in her apartments at Whitehall. At around that time, he also saw the countess of Castlemaine and Hortense Mazarin, both of whom had recently returned briefly to England.

In retrospect, it was as if he was subconsciously putting his house in order by taking leave of old friends. That night he was very restless, and on the following morning when his servants came to dress him, they found him pale, sluggish, and barely able to speak. After sitting up to be shaved, he fell back with a loud, unearthly shriek, his eyes staring ahead of him, and he was foaming at the mouth. One of his doctors, Sir Edmund King, bled and blistered him, and his head was shorn. When his speech returned, he asked for Queen Catherine to come and see him. She knelt down beside him, weeping bitterly as she rubbed his feet to try and alleviate his suffering. After a while, it proved too much for her, as she fainted and had to be gently removed to her own room by her attendants. From there she sent a message to the king, asking for his forgiveness. 'Alas! poor woman' was his reply. 'She ask my pardon? I beg hers with all my heart; take back that answer.'[67]

The duchess of Portsmouth and Nell Gwyn were not allowed any further than the king's antechamber, and thus denied a chance to say their goodbyes in person. Like the queen, the duchess also fainted, while Nell became hysterical, 'roared to a disturbance and was led out and lay roaring behind the door'. The duke of York was summoned, and he made it clear to those around them that no message should be sent to either the duke of Monmouth or the prince of Orange.

That same week, Lord Alington was fatally poisoned. It was alleged that cook and members of the household had been bribed by the duke of York or his agents. Alington was no friend of his, and if the king 'should have succumbed to any accident', he would have been a dangerous witness.[68] One of the agents in his household was under instructions to let the duke of York know as soon as he died, so he would be among the first to know and be able to tell the king. As soon as he was told, he ran to inform the king, feigning sorrow at the news, but found he had just been beaten to it by another of Alington's servants. The king said he knew, and the servant was sure he had been poisoned. 'I wish you have not a hand in it,' he told his brother solemnly, 'of which, if I were sure, you should presently go to the Tower, for I am like to be next.'[69] The duke of York told him he should not entertain such thoughts, and then admitted he was wrong to go to Scotland but agreed to do so as soon as he could, if his majesty would expedite the commission.

William Veitch was a Scottish minister, a fervent Protestant, and one of Monmouth's most loyal supporters. If his somewhat lurid account of what happened that week is to believed, then the duke of York and his supporters, having eliminated Alington, proceeded to do the same to his majesty. On the last evening of his life, they ordered generous amounts of wines, claret, and other spirits with which to keep him entertained that evening. To sober up afterwards, he was given poisoned coffee, and his snuff box was also tampered with in the same manner. When he awoke at sunrise, he felt dreadful, cried out that he was 'deadly sick', and called for his snuff box. While his servants were dressing him, he complained in agony, 'I'm gone, I'm poisoned.' Evidently expecting something of the sort, the duke of York rushed in and asked what the matter was. 'Oh, you know too well,' was the angry reply. The ailing sovereign was immediately given an antidote, but to no effect. In a fury, he tried to throw himself on his younger brother. Seeing he was in such a temper, and that the poison was not likely to work quickly, he 'set four ruffians upon him'. They choked him with his cravat and beat him soundly around the head until he died. At the dead of night, they carried him out of his chamber and buried him incognito.[70]

All of this makes a good story, but it has been dismissed by others as too far-fetched to be credible. Veitch had always been very partisan, pro-Monmouth, pro-Protestant, anti-Roman Catholic, and anti-duke of York. At various times he had left his native Scotland and lived in the north of England under the assumed names of William (or George) Johnson. He had sheltered the rebel earl of Argyll in 1681 after his escape from prison, having been sentenced to death on a dubious charge of treason following the Popish Plot, with execution suspended by Charles II 'at his pleasure'. Although he had not been directly implicated in the Rye House plot, he was among those who fled to the Dutch Republic soon afterwards. As a source, his narrative verges on the realms of conspiracy theory.

The official and generally accepted course of events, as handed down by most biographers and historians, is that King Charles lingered for several days, and the end was evidently nigh. Chronic mercury poisoning has been put forward as a likely cause, or at least a contributory factor. Always keenly interested in science, he had a had a laboratory built in the basement of the palace at Westminster, where he and his assistants would smelt, refine, and distil it, said to have been in an attempt to turn base metals into gold. He had also long been in the habit of dosing himself with mercury to ward off syphilis and other venereal infections. Kidney damage, the result of several years of fairly heavy drinking, may have been partly responsible for his demise.

All that is certain is that during the previous few years, he had been laid low with regular bouts of mild ill-health, and this time there would be no recovery.

By the afternoon of 5 February, the doctors were unsure whether he would live until the morning, and the immediate family were called to come and take their leave. Queen Catherine, the duke of York, and all his sons apart from the absent Monmouth were summoned to the bedchamber. Yet Monmouth was not forgotten, and the king asked his brother to show him clemency. Each of the boys knelt down beside the bed and he gave each one his individual blessing, as he reached out to touch them lightly on the head one last time. It was noticed that he seemed to show special fondness towards the youngest, the eleven-year-old duke of Richmond.[71]

When it was the turn of Charles, duke of St Albans, now a boy of fourteen, the king asked that a ring should be removed from his hand and presented to him. It was a gold and carnelian ring set with a likeness of King Charles I in the guise of a Roman emperor that he had taken from his finger and passed to Bishop Juxon, later archbishop of Canterbury, while on the scaffold at his execution, asking that it should be handed to his eldest son. The bishop ensured that this was done, and Charles had worn it ever since. He then put the boy's hand into that of the duke of York, asking him to take special care of his education, 'for he will be spoiled else'.[72]

In circumstances of great secrecy, the dying monarch was also received into the Roman Catholic Church by Father John Huddleston, the priest who had befriended him during his escape from Worcester after the battle in 1651. On the morning of 6 February, he asked for the curtains in front of his window to be pulled back so that he could see a sunrise for the last time, then fell into a coma and died at midday. He was fifty-four years old.

As a result of the post-mortem, his physician, Sir Charles Scarburgh, reported that the veins and arteries on the surface of the brain were unduly full; the cerebral ventricles and substance of the brain were soaked with serous fluid; the heart was large, firm, and free from malformation; the lungs, liver, kidney, and spleen were charged or engorged with blood. Some of these signified a cerebral infection, but there was no evidence of partial paralysis or a stroke, and no mention of poison of any kind. Whether he was instructed to omit anything from his statement that might have suggested foul play on the part of his brother, and that there was thus some truth in Veitch's account, there is no way of knowing.

Two of his contemporaries regarded his passing very differently. John Evelyn, who wrote that he had always found his sovereign 'ever kind [to him], and very gracious upon all occasions', lamented the passing of 'a prince of many virtues and many great imperfections'.[73] Gilbert Burnet, historian and later bishop of Salisbury, was less charitable, opining that 'he had great vices, but scarce any virtues to correct them' and that for much of his life he was 'give up to sloth and lewdness to such a degree that he hated business'.[74]

He may not have been 'a good man', yet he was shrewd as well as fortunate enough to keep his throne for nearly quarter of a century, dying in his bed in his own country. Neither his predecessor nor his successor had managed to do so. It was an achievement that both would have envied.

3

JAMES II

The swift passing of an era had taken the court by surprise. John Evelyn was among the first to sum up the general mood:

> I can never forget the inexpressible luxury and prophaneness, gaming and all dissoluteness, and as it were total forgetfulness of God (it being Sunday evening) which this date se'nnight I was witness of, the King sitting and toying with his concubines, Portsmouth, Cleveland, and Mazarin, etc., a French boy singing love songs, in that glorious gallery, whilst about 20 of the great courtiers and other dissolute persons were at basset round a large table, a bank of at least 2,000 gold before them, upon which true gentlemen who were with me made reflexions with astonishment. Six days after was all in the dust![1]

The new sovereign, James, formerly duke of York, was now King James II. One of his first actions was to send a messenger to William of Orange, asking him to apprehend the duke of Monmouth and send him to England as a prisoner. The duke had already gone to Holland at the prince's invitation some months before and was paying him a visit. He had retired to his lodgings for the night when the messenger arrived from England. When William broke the news to him of his father's death, it was recorded, 'the Duke was like one out of his senses. He was heard uttering cries and lamentations in the small house where he lodged.'[12] The news had caught him unawares as much as everyone else. In his reply to the king, William said that he was merely taking the duke of Monmouth into his protection in order to maintain the Protestant religion in England.

Monmouth still acted as if convinced that his parents had been lawfully married, that he was thus the rightful king of Britain, and that he had a mission to save the people from the 'papist regime' that his uncle seemed hellbent on creating. In this, he had the tacit, if uncertain, support of his somewhat reluctant cousin, William. Yet if he was to be exiled from Holland, in spite of sympathetic fellow exiles who had been toasting him as prince of Wales and were now lifting their glasses to King James, in other words the son but not the brother of the late King Charles, he had to find a safe haven while he considered his position. He and Henrietta planned to go to the Spanish Netherlands, perhaps in the realisation that he could turn a blind eye to those who were persuading him to try and claim the throne, put all his ambitions behind him, and lead a quieter life.

Their progress did not escape the notice of King Carlos II of Spain and his government, who had welcomed the accession of James II to the British throne and promptly ordered their arrest. Ottone Enrico dal Carretto, marquis of Grana, governor of territory, liked and sympathised with them, but he had no choice but to give Monmouth one day to escape elsewhere to safety, and Henrietta three days. The duke decided they would be safest if they returned to Holland where they might be regarded as outlaws, but at least they would be in no danger from William of Orange's men. For a while they found sanctuary with a friend who lived near Rotterdam.

Meanwhile, the duke had a staunch ally in Archibald Campbell, 9th earl of Argyll. He had been imprisoned in Scotland a few years previously on a charge of treason, was only spared execution by the intervention of Charles II, and then made good his escape to Holland. Realising that James II, his bitter enemy, would probably be quite prepared to override his brother's clemency and send him to the scaffold, he was prepared to join forces with Monmouth. His plan was to distract royal forces through a disturbance in Scotland while Monmouth intended to lead a simultaneous rising in England. He was confident of raising a force of several thousand men from his own estates, and of additional support from Presbyterian dissidents.

Monmouth had sold many of his belongings in order to raise money for arms and ships. His wife, Anne, and her mother also rose magnificently to the call for finance, pawning their jewellery in order to help him hire the Dutch warship *Helderenberg*. Heading for the south-west of England, known to be a fervently pro-Protestant area, he sailed from Holland on 30 May with a fleet of three ships, four light field guns, and about 1,500 muskets. Neither he nor Argyll had been prevented by William of Orange, who whatever his personal feelings had refrained from expressing any support for either faction.

As William was a strong supporter of the Protestant faith, one can be forgiven for thinking that whatever his views on hereditary monarchy and a preference for the natural laws of succession and therefore the duke of York as his brother's heir, a victory for his bastard nephew over his uncle and father-in-law might not have been unwelcome. He was playing a somewhat ambivalent role in proceedings, perhaps because he believed that in spite of what he might tell others, Monmouth would stop short of outright rebellion.

King Charles's illegitimate son knew that if he invaded England and lost, he could not expect any mercy. The mood of the country had changed, albeit subtly, and had resigned itself placidly if not contentedly to accepting the status quo. The climate of opinion against the 'papist' duke of York at the time of the Exclusion Crisis had more recently altered in favour of the late king's brother, who had almost been regarded as an outcast a few years earlier. Royal authority had swiftly reasserted itself after the dismissal of the last parliament, the spirit of radicalism was discredited by its association with the Rye House plot that could have plunged the country into anarchy had it not been put down by the forces of law and order, and the general mood of the populace seemed far more ready to accept the desire for a quiet life than it had at the time of King Charles I's stand against his unruly Parliamentarians. Moreover, James II's accession had taken place without a murmur of dissent, and he had recalled parliament three days after the death of Charles II. Although he was motivated more by his intention to obtain assent for generous royal income than as a sop to 'the voice of the people', he had effectively rebutted any ideas that he was intent on absolutism in the manner of his cousin over the water, King Louis XIV.

Some of the most ardent supporters of the Exclusion Bill who had considered sending the future King James into exile were among his most fervent supporters, especially if they had hopes of being appointed to the great offices of state and therefore positions of power. As a result, when

Above left: King Charles II in Garter Robes, c. 1660–65, John Michael Wright.

Above right: Lucy Walter in a shepherdess costume, c. 1657, Sir Peter Lely.

Right: Although doubts remain, this portrait is believed to be of Catherine Pegge.

Barbara Villiers, countess of Castlemaine, as Mary Magdalene, *c*. 1662, Sir Peter Lely.

Whitehall Palace, Charles II's main London residence, *c*. 1660–70.

Nell Gwyn holding a jasmine flower, Simon Verelst.

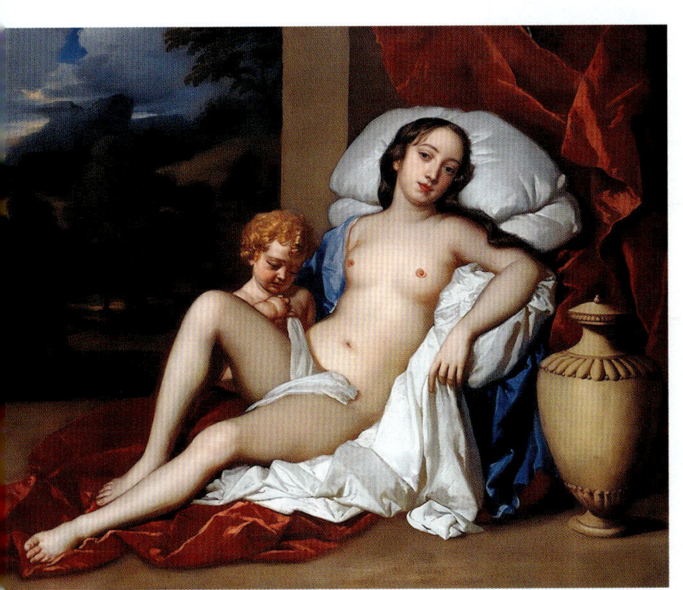

Above left: Nell Gwyn and her elder son Charles in *Venus and child*, *c.* 1671, Sir Peter Lely.

Above right: *Mary Davis*, *c.* 1670, Sir Peter Lely.

Charles and James Beauclerk, after Robert White, *c.* 1679.

Louise de Kérouaille, duchess of Portsmouth, 1672, Pierre Mignard.

Right: Charles Lennox, later duke of Richmond, as a boy, *c.* 1678.

Below: Louise de Kérouaille and her son, Charles, c. 1675, Henri Gascar.

James, duke of Monmouth, after William Wissing, *c.* 1683.

James, duke of Monmouth, in Garter Robes, Sir Peter Lely.

The Battle of Sedgemoor, 1685.

The capture of James, duke of Monmouth, from an engraving by John Quartley, 1873.

Above: The execution of the duke of Monmouth.

Left: Anne, countess of Sussex.

Charles Fitzroy, duke of Southampton, *c.* 1668, attributed to William Faithorne the Elder.

Charlotte Fitzroy, later countess of Lichfield, *c.* 1674, Sir Peter Lely.

Above left: Henry Fitzroy, duke of Grafton, *c.* 1684, Thomas Hawker.

Above right: Isabella, duchess of Grafton.

Left: Anne Scott, duchess of Buccleuch and of Monmouth, and her sons, James and Henry.

Charles Fitzroy, earl of Plymouth, *c*. 1680, after John Smith, probably after Sir Peter Lely.

Charlotte Fitzroy, later countess of Lichfield, *c*. 1700, Sir Peter Lely.

George, duke of Northumberland.

King James II, Sir Peter Lely.

Right: King William III,
Sir Godfrey Kneller.

Below: The siege of Cork, 1690,
from a contemporary print.

Above left: Lady Mary Radcliffe, daughter of Mary 'Moll' Davis, *c.* 1700, after Bernard Lens.

Above right: Diana, duchess of St Albans, *c.* 1700–19, Sir Godfrey Kneller.

Left: Charles Beauclerk, duke of St Albans, *c.* 1690, Sir Godfrey Kneller.

Charles Lennox, duke of Richmond and Lennox, *c.* 1703–10, Sir Godfrey Kneller.

Louise, duchess of Richmond, Sir Godfrey Kneller.

Above left: Charlotte Lee, countess of Lichfield, Sir Godfrey Kneller.

Above right: Louisa, countess of Berkeley, daughter of the duke of Richmond.

Sir Charles Lee, 1st earl of Lichfield, Sir Godfrey Kneller.

King James asked William to expel Monmouth from the Netherlands, the request was ignored, as if to suggest it was an unnecessary gesture because Monmouth no longer constituted a threat. To those around him, he seemed shocked and rudderless after his father's death, and in no mood to become involved in or even give his support to any rebellion.

He had reckoned without the attitudes, or even persuasion, of those around him. Foremost among these was Robert Ferguson, who had recently been appointed his army chaplain. 'The Plotter' had taken himself back to the Netherlands after the Rye House Plot, boasting that he had long been used to flight, would 'never be out of a plot' as long as he drew breath, and scoffed at his fellow-conspirators who had been less fortunate than him. When he saw that Monmouth was prevaricating and unsure of himself, he tried to stiffen his resolve. Behind the duke's back, he condemned him for 'his great numbness of spirit and slothfulness'.[3]

To his face, the chaplain was persuasiveness personified. Asserting that King Charles II had indeed been poisoned, he impressed on Monmouth that he had a sacred duty to act, to do his sacred duty on behalf of the Protestants in the British kingdoms, saving them from 'nothing less than the eradication of their freedoms and religion'. If he was to act, the circumstances would be favourable, and the people would rise as one to support him. The earl of Argyll was in charge of the pro-Protestant forces in Scotland, he was confident of success, and his support would be invaluable. Yet only if Monmouth committed himself to the venture would he do likewise.

Surrounded by voices who eagerly urged him on, Monmouth had no alternative but to commit himself to an invasion in which he would be heavily reliant on good luck. He, Ferguson, and his supporters sailed from Holland and came into harbour at Lyme Regis, Dorset, on 11 June. 'The Plotter' Ferguson had prepared a long proclamation denouncing King James as a usurper and a tyrant, and for having poisoned his brother in order to hasten his succession to the throne. It was an accusation that would come back to haunt Monmouth in his final hours. The document was read out in full to the people on the town hall steps.

On their first day, he and his followers recruited about 300 additional supporters. King James's intelligence had been aware that they were on their way from mainland Europe, and the town mayor, Gregory Alford, informed the local militias. Two customs officers were sent to ride to London and warn the authorities. A force was assembled, led by

John Churchill and Louis de Duras, earl of Feversham, a former lord chamberlain to Queen Catherine. By 15 June, Monmouth's army had swelled to over 1,000 men. Over the next few days, he recruited more, although most of the agricultural workers were armed with nothing better than pitchforks. A proclamation hailing him as king was made, and an improvised coronation was staged in Taunton on 20 June. Some of his supporters, who were anti-Catholic but more or less republican in nature and may have anticipated another Commonwealth without a monarch, were not impressed. Meanwhile, the royal forces under Churchill and Feversham swelled with the aid of reinforcements from London, continued to close in on him, while the navy captured Monmouth's ships to ensure any escape route back to the continent would be sealed.

Monmouth's main objective seemed to be an attack on Bristol. The verdict of some historians is that had he and his men arrived there a few days earlier, while it was only protected by the Gloucestershire militia, he would have had a good chance of taking the city, attracted far more followers, and the final outcome might have been different. Each day, more troops loyal to King James converged on the area, gradually gaining the upper hand.

Among them was a contingent of cavalry and musketeers, led by Monmouth's half-brother, the countess of Castlemaine's son, Henry, duke of Grafton. Feversham placed him in command of a large troop of horse and musketeers. On 27 June, he led about 500 musketeers on a potentially hazardous reconnaissance through a narrow lane being barricaded by the rebels in the village of Norton St Philip, where they came under heavy fire from the rebels. About eighty were shot dead, but the rest escaped by charging through them with fixed bayonets and forcing their way directly through the lane until they reached the fields beyond. Yet the rebels suffered far less casualties, losing only about twenty men in the fight. Grafton's horse was shot under him, and he was fortunate to escape unscathed. It was the last success that Monmouth's men would enjoy.

During the next few days, the two opposing forces cautiously watched each other from a distance. It had been rash, if not complacent, of Monmouth to rely too much on any success his allies north of the border might have had. The morale of his forces began to crumble when news of Argyll's failure reached them. His Scottish ally, on whose success he had pinned so many hopes, had sailed from Holland at the beginning of May with a force of about 300 men. The venture was a complete fiasco; Argyll was a brave, but inexperienced commander, and the rebel leaders under him could not agree among themselves. After a failed attempt to invade the Scottish Lowlands, most of them were soon captured and several were executed. Argyll was among them, and after being held in Edinburgh Castle for a few days, he ascended the scaffold on 30 June.

There was no sign, or even any news, of impending cavalry reinforcements from elsewhere, or tidings of a possible Protestant uprising in Cheshire that had been vaguely mentioned some days earlier. The rebels were increasingly exhausted, footsore, tired, and hungry, still marching to keep ahead of the royal army, and having to camp in waterlogged fields at night. Some of his men, fearing the whole enterprise was doomed, began to drift away. The remaining army held a council of war, at which they suggested that that the men should be allowed to take the benefit of the pardon offered by the king to any who wished to desert at this stage, and all the others should make good their escape as best they could.

Monmouth might have saved himself at this stage. Yet he was reluctant to abandon his campaign, especially as he had experience of the way that King James dealt with plotters and believed that nobody could have any faith in whatever assurances he might offer. A few tried to persuade him to cut his losses and escape while he could, but after hesitating, he decided there was no choice but to keep on to the bitter end. Those who knew him were aware of his tendency to vacillate, and his inability to make decisions. As King James would later remark in one of his kindlier moments, 'Poor Monmouth, he was always easy to be imposed upon.'[4]

Feversham had no difficulty in keeping the rebels in the westcountry under close watch until the rest of his forces arrived. Among them were three battalions of British mercenaries that had been sent from Holland by William of Orange. Until then, his actions had suggested those of a man who had probably been keeping his eye on a safe distance to see who would be the winner: King James or his nephew. One cannot resist the thought that he may have been taking the longer view in predicting, or at least taking a gamble on, the likely outcome, aware that circumstances favoured the new king as the more probable victor in the short term. His intelligence sources had been keeping him informed, and they presumably advised him that the rebels' chances were looking more slender by the day. It was only to be expected that the obstinately papist James might be a cautious sovereign at first, bide his time, but ultimately antagonise the nation and then be driven off the throne before long. Should this happen, it would be easier to help drive him out (or even put himself at the head of such a campaign) than displace the Protestant and perhaps by then well-entrenched Monmouth on the throne. It was certainly not in William's interests to see Britain upset the balance of power in Europe by allying herself with a mighty Catholic France just the other side of the Channel.

Feversham had been biding his time, but on 30 June, his additional troops and artillery arrived in Somerset. Having failed to take Bristol, Monmouth had no choice but to fall back on Bridgwater. All escape routes that had been open to him were now blocked by the royal army encamped on Sedgemoor. His only chance lay in launching an attack when it was least expected.

Overnight on 5–6 July, Monmouth decided to gamble on personally leading a surprise night-time assault on his adversaries. It might have succeeded had it not been for a shot fired from a passing royalist patrol, or as has been rumoured, a traitor within his ranks while they were still about a mile from the royal camp. His bold attempt to take the foe unawares had failed. Battle had been joined and he sent his cavalry ahead to engage them at once, with the foot soldiers following as quickly as they could. During the pitched battle, Churchill was in control of the royal forces with Grafton his second-in-command, conducting himself, it was said, 'with all imaginable resolution and bravery'.

The duke of Monmouth's enthusiastic, but ramshackle band of volunteers, mostly poorly armed farmers and agricultural workers, were no match for the numerically slightly smaller, but far better equipped, properly trained, and disciplined soldiers that attacked them at first light on three sides. The rebels were soundly defeated, with many of the men cut down by cannon and musket fire, and estimated losses of about 1,300 killed, while the royalists lost 200 men, perhaps less. About 500 of Monmouth's men were captured and imprisoned in St Mary's Parish Church, Westonzoyland, while others were hunted and shot in the ditches where they were hiding or hanged from gibbets erected along the roadside. Many of those who had escaped were captured and tried in the Bloody Assizes, with 1,300 found guilty and either executed or transported abroad.

It was one of Monmouth's many misfortunes not to meet a courageous death in the thick of battle and die like a true hero, fighting for what he perceived to be his inheritance. He was among those who escaped, and a reward of £5,000 was offered for his capture. Gaunt, starving, unshaven, and disguised as a shepherd, he was discovered two days later in a ditch near Ringwood in the New Forest. The soldiers who found him identified him by the Order of St George that was found in his pocket. Had he discarded it on his flight, he might have survived. Instead, he was arrested and taken to London to meet his inevitable fate.

On the day of his capture, the children from his marriage were also sent to the Tower, to prevent the possibility of their becoming figureheads for any possible future uprising in his name. The duchess went with them, and she met the duke that evening in his cell, in the presence of Henry, earl of Clarendon, lord privy seal. He received them coldly, complaining that she had not done the part of a wife towards him at the late king's (his father's) death, and told her he thought she did not show any great concern for him under his present misfortunes and did not seem to want to speak to her. During their conversation, he addressed himself to the latter rather than to his estranged wife, mentioning his hopes that his majesty would show him mercy. She angrily interrupted him and told him that he was deluding himself if he imagined he was going to be spared. She insisted that he must sign a statement affirming that she and the children had nothing to do with his rebellion and had not the slightest association with the sympathetic Whig opposition.

He seemed much happier by now with Lady Harriet Wentworth, with whom he admitted he had lived the last two years as man and wife. The duchess, he said, 'was imposed upon him when he was very young and not by his own choice, and that she was his wife in law, but the other was his wife before God and in his own conscience'. Before he died, they persuaded him to speak to the duchess and his children, 'which he did more freely than the day before, and charged his son to obey his mother, who would carefully bring him up in the Protestant religion, and thus he took his leave of them'.[5]

On 13 June, parliament passed an Act of Attainder, sentencing him to death as a traitor, thus dispensing with the necessity for a trial. The next day, King James allowed him an audience, despite having no intention of granting him a pardon, contrary to the tradition that the sovereign would give an audience only when he intended to show clemency. Monmouth begged for forgiveness and offered to convert to Catholicism if he was spared, but the king was disgusted by his abject behaviour and told him to prepare to meet his maker. Pleas to the king including one from his sister-in-law, Dowager Queen Catherine, were ignored. A kinder man might have sent him to the Tower, but James was determined to make an example of him, especially as a rival who still commanded widespread support would remain a potential focus for opposition and inspiration for further uprisings as long as he lived. Above all, he had committed the unpardonable crime in launching an invasion against the lawful monarch.

According to Sir John Bramston, the lawyer and politician:

> I have been told the King asked him how he could expect pardon that had used him so, 'To make me a murderer and poisoner of my dear brother, besides all the other villainies you charge me with in your declaration'. To which Monmouth replied, 'Ferguson drew it and made me sign it before ever I read it'. That so angered the King that he said, 'This is trifling: would you sign a paper of such consequence and not read it?' So he turned from him and bid him prepare to die.[6]

James reported in a letter to William that the duke 'seemed more concerned and desirous to live, and did not behave himself so well as I expected nor as one ought to have expected from one who had taken upon him to be King.' In view of such a scathing verdict, it was surprising to note that his majesty had also highly commended Monmouth's generalship in his abortive attempt at conquest, saying 'he had not made one false step'.[7]

All the same, there was to be no reprieve for the man whose sentence of death had been scheduled to take place at Tower Hill on 15 July. Some Tudor executions, notably that of Lady Jane Grey in 1554, had been carried out privately within the Tower, but James, duke of Monmouth, was to be denied this privilege. As he was about to take his last steps towards the scaffold, two bishops came to see him and prepare him for eternity. Yet they would not let him take the Eucharist, as he refused to acknowledge that either his rebellion against King James or his relationship with Lady Wentworth had been a sin. Another clergyman encouraged him to die like a Christian, tell the crowds that he stood before them as an example of rebellion, and beg them and the people to be loyal to his majesty, but he angrily refused.

Facing the crowds, he proclaimed that he was going to die as a Protestant of the Church of England. When he was asked to denounce his invasion as an act of rebellion, he said nothing but instead handed over his confession on a piece of paper. It expressed his regret at having been declared king, 'and confirmed that he knew his parents had never been married'. There was no statement of loyalty or penitence to King James II, whom he called 'the king who is now', and he asked only that the same person would not punish his children on his account after he was gone.[8]

As he prepared to lay his head on the block, he told Jack Ketch, the executioner, to do his business well and finish him with one blow. He had no wish to suffer like Lord Russell, whom he had beheaded two years earlier for his part in the Rye House plot, and who was only dispatched after at least two or three clumsy efforts. Unnerved, Ketch again failed to carry his duty out efficiently and found he would need to inflict multiple blows with his axe, much to the horror of the crowds who had gathered to witness the occasion. Eventually he threw down his axe in despair and had to finish the gory job off with a knife.

The dead man was buried in the Church of St Peter ad Vincula in the Tower of London. King James, or rather his forces, had triumphed on one of the last battlefields in English history, but in a sense, it would prove his undoing. For the next three years, he acted as though his last enemy was vanquished, he was firmly entrenched, and his throne was secure at last. It would lose him the considerable goodwill of parliament he had inherited on his accession and taken for granted, and then the confidence and affection of the nation.[9]

*****

On his deathbed, King Charles had asked the duke of York to ensure that Nell Gwyn, the duchess of Portsmouth, and their children should be properly provided for when he was gone.

The French mistress would fare less well than the English one. Although relations had cooled between the king and the duchess, she made her peace with him in his last months, and he spent the occasional relaxed evening with her about a week before he died. His health had been indifferent for some time, but even so she was taken aback by the suddenness of his passing, especially as he had seemed well enough until the final week. She suspected that their son, Charles, duke of Richmond, might have an uncertain life ahead of him. With this in mind she therefore took the precaution shortly before his father's death to have him naturalised as a French subject, and the official patent was registered on 22 January 1685. It proved to be just in time, for just a fortnight later, King Charles II was no more.

James liked neither the duchess of Portsmouth nor her son. Much to her annoyance, he stripped the twelve-year-old of his office as master of the horse, saying that it was quite inappropriate as a small boy would be incapable of performing such duties and they would have to be carried out by a deputy. Nevertheless, she promised him that she would persuade her young son to enter the Roman Catholic Church, probably considering that with his capricious uncle on the throne, it would be for his own good. King James was pleased, and he promised that he would protect him 'with all his power'.[10]

Yet she realised that with her protector now gone, she would no longer be welcome in England. She had accrued considerable debts, and the creditors that had hesitated to demand repayment during the reign of Charles II would be much less likely to hold back now he was gone. She was not well liked in England, and verbal attacks on her in parliament made it clear that she would do better to absent herself. The only really safe place for her and her son, it seemed, would be France. She had already been created Duchesse d'Aubigny, and her son would surely succeed to the dukedom after her death. King Charles had given the duke of Richmond an allowance of £3,000 and awarded her one of £2,000, but she asked that both payments should be made in the name of her son. He had revenues from the confiscated estates of Lord Grey in Ireland, but it would not be possible for him to draw on these until he was an adult.

When she reminded King James that his brother had promised her 'something from Ireland', he ignored her. Embittered comments she made about him soon reached his ears and made him only less inclined to help. Yet when she announced that she would be leaving England that summer, he looked on her more favourably, especially as he knew that King Louis XIV would not be well-disposed towards him if she complained of ill-treatment at his hands. He went to see her, promised to keep an eye on the interests of herself and her son, talked kindly to his nephew, and again encouraged him to become a Roman Catholic. Mother and son heard him out in silence.

Once she had paid off her debts in England, she and Richmond arrived in France in August, six months after King Charles's death. With them went her jewellery and 200,000 francs that she had been granted on the death of King Charles. King Louis liked his half-English kinsman immediately, and even more when later that year he attended a mass in the king's presence and affirmed that he was a member of the Roman

Catholic church. He was so delighted that he gave the duchess an increase in pension to 20,000 livres. It was vital for her to retain his goodwill. She had hardly had a chance to settle down in her new home when she sent her son to pay his respects to the king, who received him graciously. She knew well what importance the monarch and Madame de Maintenon, his morganatic wife, attached to individual conversions of this nature, and she had been preparing with some care for the boy's change of religion ever since the death of Charles II. He was given the necessary instruction with all haste, and the ceremony took place at Fontainebleau in the king's presence on 21 October.

With due regard for the rank and birth of Charles's son, the French sovereign intended everything to take place before the passing of such a potentially draconian anti-Protestant measure, and to be conducted in an appropriately solemn character. Next day, he was to sign the revocation of the Edict of Nantes and replace it with the Edict of Fontainebleau. This declared the Protestant faith illegal and led to the destruction of Huguenot churches and the closure of Protestant schools, as well as resulting in the flight of thousands from France to other countries in Europe and beyond.

It would be the start of a restless life for the duke of Richmond, who was still not yet on the threshold of adult life. He remained in France for about a year, but then realised that there seemed no chance of any privileged position at the French court and returned to London. Much to his irritation, King James made it plain that he had no intention of helping him embark on a military career, let alone any of the privileges to which he believed himself entitled as the sovereign's nephew.

The duchess of Portsmouth had been unlucky, but the late sovereign's deathbed instruction to his brother 'Let not poor Nelly starve' was faithfully observed. Nell Gwyn had always been liked and was remarkably free of enemies. King James appointed new trustees to handle her financial affairs, granted her an annual pension of £1,500, paid off most of her debts, and also the mortgage on her Nottinghamshire lodge Bestwood, which remained in the Beauclerk family until 1940. A year later, Burford House was leased to Prince George of Denmark, husband of the king's younger surviving daughter, Anne.

These arrangements ensured that she should want for little in her remaining years, but these turned out to be less than anyone might have imagined. Moreover, the favours did not come without strings. The king strongly suggested that she ought to dismiss the duke of St Albans's Protestant tutor in favour of a Catholic, surround themselves with Catholics in their household, and to convert to the Roman Catholic faith themselves. He reminded her that King Charles had done so shortly before his death, and that he had entrusted him as his heir and successor with the boy's education.

Nell shared the general distrust of papism and refused to be bullied. Not used to being thwarted in this way, King James dropped hints that his nephew's inheritance could be at risk if she did not comply. Her health was already far from good, and the resultant stress in his attempts to coerce her probably contributed to her illness. After a stroke in March 1687, she became paralysed on one side, and two months later a second left her confined to bed in her Pall Mall house. She lingered for another six months, taking comfort in the fact that her son had defied the king and refused to change her religion, and that thanks to the generosity of Dowager Queen Catherine, he would be paid an annual pension from her own funds of £2,000.

On 14 November, she died from apoplexy, perhaps exacerbated by syphilis, at the early age of thirty-seven. Chief among her bequests was a large estate, including Burford House, near Windsor Castle. She may not have been granted the title she possibly longed for, but some two and a half centuries later, she would be remembered in a way unique to mistresses of British royalty. In 1937, a newly completed, ten-storey block of flats in Sloane Avenue, Chelsea, was named Nell Gwyn House. A high alcove above the main entrance contains a statue of her, with a Cavalier King Charles spaniel at her feet.

*****

From the last days of King Charles onwards, the countess of Castlemaine had two partners, both of whom turned out to be thoroughly unfortunate choices. The first was Cardell (or Cardonell) Goodman, whose date of birth was uncertain, but he was probably at least ten, perhaps as much as fifteen years younger than her. He was an actor by profession, and he was deemed by some to have been a remarkably undistinguished one. So many details of his life seem to be shrouded in mystery, and it is difficult to draw a line between fact, hearsay, and fiction. Earlier in life he had supposedly inherited £2,000 on his father's death, a considerable sum for those days, but squandered it before he took to the stage.

On 27 October 1684, he pleaded not guilty at the Court of King's Bench to a charge of conspiring and endeavouring to hire an agent to poison the dukes of Grafton and Northumberland. At his trial on 7 November at Westminster he was convicted, and seventeen days later, he was sentenced to pay a fine of £1,000 'and find sureties for his good behaviour for life'.[11] One version of events is that the brothers, who had much in common and would remain close until the elder's early death, knew that Goodman was a blackguard of low birth, would bring their mother nothing but misery, and they were desperate to try and end the relationship by any means possible. One way was to accuse him of highway robbery, an offence for which he had apparently been caught and convicted in the past. Another was to charge him with a conspiracy to kill them, murder by poison being easier to get away with than attacking and shooting or stabbing them.

So, did they themselves conspire to have him tried and convicted of a serious crime in the hope that it would end his chances of becoming their father-in-law? If that is the case, it evidently failed. In spite of his supposed guilt, she continued to see him, and according to some sources, she gave birth to a son by him in March 1686. Nothing is known of this child, and it may be no more than idle rumour. There are grounds for supposing that Goodman witnessed a deed involving some of her property the following year, but by this time, the affair had probably run its course. It would not, however, be the last the judiciary had heard of him.

*****

After the death of his father, the duke of Grafton's relationship with the crown was bound to change. King James liked and respected his nephew, with none of the mutual distrust that had arisen between him and Monmouth. Although Grafton was a personable, outgoing character, very unlike the dour James, both men got on well. At the coronation at Westminster Abbey on 23 April, he officiated as lord high constable. This was a ceremonial office that was revived only for coronations and was concerned with certain formalities that formed part of the proceedings, but it was a significant honour all the same.

On 19 November 1685, he first took his seat in the House of Lords. Nevertheless, within a few weeks, he would be in trouble. On New Year's Day 1686, he attended an entertainment hosted by the duke of Shrewsbury and his family, and his brother, John Talbot, had given Grafton some 'unhandsome and provoking language'. Talbot had danced in a shroud at the gathering. Not long before that, he was forewarned that he 'should be killed by a tall black man before he was twenty-one years old'.[12] Both men subsequently fought a duel a month later, on 2 February, at Chelsea. According to Peregrine Bertie, a son of the earl of Lindsay, a vice-chamberlain at court:

> Poor Mr. Talbot was run through the heart and fell dead upon the place. The Duke was saved by a little buckle belonging to his belt, or some little picture he wore about him. It seems they both thrust at the same time, Mr. Talbot's sword hitting on the buckle missed going through the Duke's body and ripped up his side.[13]

Within a few days, Grafton was granted a pardon by the king, but he still thought it prudent to go into hiding in order to escape any possible retribution from Talbot's friends. However, it seems that he emerged a few days later, when history repeated itself. On 19 February, according to John Evelyn:

> Many bloody and notorious duels were fought about this time. The Duke of Grafton killed Mr Stanley, brother to the Earl of [Derby], indeed upon an almost insufferable provocation. It is to be hoped that His Majesty will at last severely remedy this unchristian custom.[14]

Grafton was known to have an uncertain temper, and evidently suffered neither fools nor gratuitous insults gladly. The king apparently let 'this unchristian custom' pass unchecked, and nothing was done. Duelling had been suppressed, though not completely eliminated, during the Cromwellian era when the Parliamentarians' Articles of War advocated the death penalty for would-be combatants, but after the Restoration, it went unchecked. While all the Stuart monarchs heartily disliked it and made their views known, they never did anything to control it, let alone give their encouragement to those who wished to curtail the activity, as by then it was so entrenched among the aristocracy. The duke prudently laid low for a short time, then emerged to play a strange role relating to the recent marriage of his brother the duke of Northumberland, which caused some ill-feeling at the time but was soon smoothed over and forgiven.

Northumberland had become betrothed to Catherine Wheatley, the widow of Thomas Lucy, a captain in the Horse Guards, and daughter of Robert Wheatley, a poulterer from Bracknell, and they were married on 8 April 1685. Grafton was angry to find out about his younger brother's nuptials. She was poor, Grafton protested, and while he admitted she might be beautiful, being the daughter of a simple tradesman, her humble background meant that she was not good enough for his brother. Evelyn recorded in his diary that Northumberland, 'marrying very meanly, with the help of his brother Grafton, attempted in vain to spirit away his wife'.[15] Grafton kidnapped them both, forcing Northumberland to send her to Flanders and place her in a convent in Ghent, as it seemed the most appropriate way of separating him from a wife he considered unsuitable. Having seen his orders carried out, Grafton sought consultation with lawyers with regard to obtaining a divorce for the couple.

In fact, at first it was possible that, rather than the brothers consulting the legal profession for correcting what one of them viewed as a cardinal error, both of them might be taken to court for taking the law into their own hands and trying to remedy the issue so clumsily themselves.

Peregrine Bertie wrote to Lady Rutland in some excitement of a report being received as confirming the safe arrival of the two dukes at Ostende: 'As soon as they return they will be taken into custody by the Lord Chief Justice's warrant and must give bail for their appearance or go to prison.' Within a few days, it was concluded that some compromise must have been reached, as no more was said of the affair beyond a note in a letter to the duke of Albemarle: 'Our two Dukes of Grafton and Northumberland are returned from Flanders, where they have left the new Duchess in a nunnery. They say she was willing to stay, and her friends here are willing she should do so.'[16]

King James II had intended that Northumberland should marry a daughter of Henry Cavendish, 2nd duke of Newcastle. He was also initially displeased at his nephew's choice of bride, but on reflection he was prepared to consider it binding and recognise it as a *fait accompli*. Moreover, he was angry with Grafton's high-handed treatment of the new duchess of Northumberland, especially after members of her family complained, and he ordered the brothers to bring her back to England so she could be presented at court. When they returned, she was welcomed, and in June 1686, she was made a lady of the bedchamber to Queen Mary.

A contemporary and anonymous versifier satirised Northumberland's behaviour:

Northumberland now to his trial stood forth,
And pleaded the preference due to his birth;
No fool he did hope, howe'er eminent, would
Presume to compare with a fool of the blood.

Appealing besides to his scandalous marriage,
His beautiful face, and his dull stupid carriage,
To a soul without sense of truth, honour, or wit,
If e'er man was formed for a woman so fit.

But his prince-like project to kidnap his wife,
And a lady so free to make pris'ner for life;
Was tyranny to which the sex ne'er would submit,
And an ill-natured fool they liked worse than a wit.

Another of the poets produced 'A song to the tune of taking old snuff is the mode of the Court', which also made fun of the ducal goings-on:

Since his grace could prefer
The poulterer's heir
To the great match his uncle had made him;
'Twere just if the King
Took away his blue string,
And sewed him on two to lead him.

That the lady was sent
To a convent at Ghent,
Was the counsel of kidnapping Grafton;
And we now may foretell,
That all will go well,
Since the rough blockhead governs the soft one.[17]

The duke of Grafton was considered to be the king's favourite nephew and was evidently held in high regard. The king appointed him vice-admiral of the Narrow Seas, which involved responsibility for the naval command of the English navy's operating in the seas between England, France, and Holland for a couple of years. As a result, he was entrusted with some important missions during the next couple of years. On 3 July 1687, he escorted the papal envoy, Ferdinando d'Adda, to Whitehall. Adda had been sent by Pope Innocent XI as Papal Nuncio in London, charged with persuading King James to intercede with King Louis XIV, with whom as a Catholic he was on the best of terms, to modify his attitude towards the persecuted Protestants in France.

Within two days of his return to England, he took command of the fleet to escort Maria Sophia of Neuburg, the Princess Palatine, from Rotterdam to Lisbon, where she was to be married to Pedro II, king of Portugal. Flying his flag in the *Anne*, he took charge when she departed from Den Brielle in the Netherlands on 12 July and sailed for Portugal. Fierce winds at the mouth of the Channel delayed them briefly and they had to put into Plymouth until conditions had improved. On their way, they had an encounter with another ship of which they were initially a little suspicious. He detached two of the frigates, *Hampshire* and *Sedgemoor*, to investigate. It turned out that she was the *Orange Tree*, from Algiers, a new ship of forty guns with 350 men on board, with the brother-in-law of the Dey of Algiers in command. Once the British Navy had produced their pass signed by the English consul, the ships parted with the customary friendly returning salutes.

Grafton and his fleet arrived at Lisbon on 1 August. As the representative of one of Portugal's most time-honoured allies, the duke himself was accorded special treatment by a grateful King Pedro:

> The Master of the King's household was sent to escort his Grace the Duke of Grafton ashore to an apartment provided for him, which he excused upon the directions he had from his Majesty to continue on board. On August 4th His Grace had his audience of His Majesty, which was deemed then a particular mark of esteem, none of the foreign ministers having been till after that time admitted to see the King. Don Juan de Souza was sent to bring the Duke in one of the King's barges, the Portuguese Men-of-War saluting him as they passed. The Duke, with Mr Fitzjames [James Fitzjames, duke of Berwick, son of James II and Arabella

> Churchill] and Lord O'Brien, the commanders of the squadron, and the other gentlemen, landing at the new bridge made for the Queen, were conducted to the King's apartment, the guards standing at arms and the drums beating. His Grace was welcomed by the King with great kindness, and his compliments returned with large expressions, how sensible the King was of the marks of his Majesty's friendship, particularly of his last obliging instance of it in sending his Grace to conduct the Queen. The Duke then presenting Mr Fitzjames, the King directed himself more particularly to him, and received also very kindly Lord O'Brien, the Commanders of the ships and the rest that were presented to his Majesty at the same time. Thence the Duke was conducted to his audiences of the Queen and Infanta; none being admitted with him but Mr. Fitzjames and the officers belonging to the ceremony; which being done, they were all carried in the King's coaches to the Palace, where there was a very noble entertainment provided, the King's servants attending, and on the same night there was a great quantity of all sorts of fresh provisions sent on board to be distributed among the ships. The Duke had several other invitations given him, all which he excused. On the 8th the King's presents were sent, which were a sword and cane set with diamonds for the Duke and a jewel of value for Mr Fitzjames. On the 10th his Grace was conducted to his audiences of leave with the same ceremonies and entertainments.[18]

Duly gratified by the hospitality he had received, Grafton and his fleet left the Portuguese capital on 13 August and sailed for Gibraltar. While they were there, a French squadron under the Comte de Tourville, one of King Louis XIV's senior naval officers, entered the bay, and the commanders exchanged complimentary visits. With a more ardently pro-Catholic sovereign on the British throne, the French were keen to see some signs of closer cooperation between both countries in the years ahead.

Next on the programme, matters on the north coast of Africa were about to claim Grafton's attention. British involvement with Tangier had come to an end in 1684 because of the expense of maintaining it as a colonial outpost, but her naval interests in the Mediterranean were undiminished. King Charles had always appreciated the importance of keeping a naval presence there, a policy that his successor endorsed. Grafton was clearly the obvious person to help or play an active role in this. As king and government were careful not to arouse any suspicion among the Mediterranean powers, it was vital to observe a degree of secrecy with regard to the fleet's destination until the last possible moment. As far as other European nations and rulers were concerned, the official line was that the duke of Grafton was planning to take a cruise around the Channel Islands. Only close observers were aware that the number of ships assembled and amounts of stores on board at Portsmouth obviously pointed to a far grander venture than that, and that it was not entirely coincidental that Grafton had been appointed admiral of the fleet on 5 July.

Their immediate destination was Algiers, where they arrived on 17 September. Here the duke was received with great respect and attention by the Dey, Mezzomorto, who gave him 'every assurance of his wish to continue in peace and friendship with the English and presenting him with several English persons who had been made prisoners during the former war'. Although it went unnoticed at the time, in a case heard before the House of Lords six years later, it appeared that one of the parties, having suffered detention and the confiscation of his ship at the hands of the Dey, owed his release to the duke. His attention had been drawn to the man's plight, and once informed, 'manned his boat and sent to the Governor demanding the surrender of the man, which so alarmed the country', that he was released forthwith.[19]

Grafton set sail again on 6 October. At Tunis, and then at Tripoli, he received similar honours and met with the same success. During the journey, he made a detour to Cagliari in the island of Sardinia to take in fresh water. Here the viceroy, the duke of Monteleone, a Neapolitan, honoured Mr Fitzjames by receiving him with the discharge of twenty-one guns. When he learned that it was the king's birthday, he wanted to mark it with a great entertainment and a ball, to which he would have invited the duke of Grafton and his principal officers. However, as there was a good wind after a recent period of storms, the admiral with his habitual sense of nautical duty insisted on sailing that evening, his departure being saluted with the discharge of forty pieces of cannon.

Having successively renewed England's existing treaties with Algiers, Tunis, and Tripoli, he prepared to sail for home. They anchored at Malta on 19 November, where he was made a knight of St John. On his return voyage, at Malta, at Messina, at Malaga, and at every other port where the squadron touched, the governors and inhabitants of each place seemed to be competing with each other as to which could most distinguish themselves by the honour and attention paid to the royal representative.

They went from Messina to Malaga via Leghorn, where their arrival was saluted by the discharge of 100 guns. At Malaga, the party from the fleet was received on landing by the Governor and magistrates with a dozen coaches, a guard of honour of thirty horse and the town militia consisting of eight companies. A reception was held at the consul's house and on the governor's departure, the bishop of Malaga, with several persons of the first rank and quality, presented themselves. The official visits were subsequently returned, and the governor completed his courtesies by sending on board a generous present of fresh provisions.

When they arrived at Gibraltar, Grafton was greeted with the news that Queen Mary was expecting another child. As five of her previous ten pregnancies had ended in stillbirths or produced children who died in early infancy, there was little reason to suspect that their fortunes might change for the better this time. However, Grafton was prepared to welcome the news, 'and for joy thereof (he) commanded the same evening that all the ships should fire their cannon, which being done the commanders came on board the Duke to express their congratulations upon this solemn occasion'.[20]

When the fleet returned to England on 19 March 1688, he received a fulsome welcome home from the king, no less flattering than those given him by the foreign nations he had been visiting. In a voyage lasting nearly nine months, often during bad weather, he had crossed 5,000 miles of sea without the loss of any ships or even any substantial damage. He had thoroughly relished all these missions as the representative of the British crown, especially as he loved the sea and enjoyed overseas travelling from an early age.

Yet how strong his attachment or rather loyalty had ever been to King James II was open to question. By the summer of 1688, the latter's hold on his throne was looking increasingly tenuous. The British were prepared to accept a Roman Catholic on the throne, but not one who wilfully gave Catholics preferment in official life, and in the army and navy. English and Scottish parliaments refused to pass his measures at will. Whereas his brother would have conceded gracefully, James tried to impose by decree. In his refusal to compromise, he showed he was his father's son. Having gradually forfeited goodwill and lost support throughout his reign, he weakened his position fatally in the summer of 1688.

Any British hopes of seeing the succession pass peacefully on his death to his elder daughter, Mary, wife of the prince of Orange and a devout Anglican, were dashed, temporarily at least, when Queen Mary gave birth to a son, James Francis Edward. There were rumours that the child had not been fathered by the king, who was believed by some to be impotent after an attack of venereal disease some years earlier, and that another newly born infant had been smuggled into the palace. Unlike the couple's previous sickly sons, he was not only born alive but throve, thus making a Catholic succession almost inevitable.

His appearance in the nursery was followed almost immediately by the ill-considered prosecution of the 'Seven Bishops' for seditious libel, regarded as an attack on the Church of England. The nationwide celebrations that followed their acquittal astonished the king and proved beyond doubt that he had not only gradually squandered much of the goodwill that had been accorded to him on his accession, but also that his authority over the kingdom now counted for next to nothing.

For a short period, it looked as if a reign might end in Civil War for the second time in less than forty years. By the end of June, the prince of Orange had been invited to invade England with his army, and within three months he was ready to set sail. The embattled King James's support had begun to melt away visibly by the time his son-in-law landed at Brixham, on the coast of Devon, and he sent word to various military officers in London whom he believed were still loyal. Among them were John Churchill, later earl (and later still duke) of Marlborough, and Grafton, and they all gave him their word that they would fight and die for the sovereign. It would soon prove a hollow assurance.

At first Grafton, who remained unflinchingly loyal for the moment, believed he was the perfect candidate to be put in overall command of the fleet getting ready to set out later in 1688 to guard against William of Orange's invasion force. But in September, James appointed Dartmouth over his head once again, creating for him the new post of admiral of the fleet, in other words the senior officer in overall charge. He also abolished the office of vice-admiral of England altogether, a move that one observer in the fleet regarded as a subtle move to be rid of the duke. Grafton was not only much less experienced, but he was also strongly opposed to the promotion of Catholics in army and navy, as well as the king's francophile foreign policy, and had told James this to his face. Moreover, his role in the recent Northumberland marriage business may have been forgiven, but it hinted that there was something of the wild youth about him that made him less dependable than a veteran officer about fifteen years his senior.

Dartmouth, one of James's most loyal supporters, had his suspicions about the duke. While writing to his majesty on 22 October about the victualling of the fleet and the filling up of stores, felt impelled to discuss the general state of matters. He had some 'hints of dissatisfaction in some young men', he noted, mentioning one or two that he felt could not be trusted, adding that Grafton 'was down here among them a little after my coming, though he would not let me know it'.[21]

Grafton had been a close friend of John Churchill since the Sedgemoor campaign, and both had various contacts in what gave every appearance of a slowly unfolding army conspiracy. There had been no doubt as to his commitment to James's army at the time of the Battle of Sedgemoor and during the two years afterwards at least, when he swore that he would fight and die for his sovereign. Yet Feversham suspected that his support could not be taken for granted. He had warned the king to beware of Grafton, Churchill, and others including Prince George of Denmark, who all seemed to be wavering. Grafton had recently paid what was meant to be a secret visit to William in Holland. It came to the notice of James's agents, and they duly reported it back to him, but he realised it would be futile to take any action. Grafton then went to the fleet at least once, ostensibly as a volunteer. At one stage, probably in late October, there were conspiratorial murmurings throughout the fleet with a view to kidnapping Dartmouth while he was dining aboard ship commanded by Anthony Hastings, an experienced naval officer who also held a commission in Grafton's regiment.

When a council of officers was held in London on the eve of the king's departure for Salisbury, Grafton made a passionate appeal to them for their loyalty. Yet his heart may no longer have been completely in it by then. There was, however, more to his behaviour than merely acting as a turncoat because he wanted to be on the winning side. As a scion of the house of Stuart and a public servant, he could see the advantages of following the established order of succession as endorsed by his father in retaining King James on the throne, but at the same time appreciate that if the king's policies and attitude were endangering the crown or running the risk of civil war for the second time within less than fifty years, there was nothing to be gained by sticking doggedly to a path that could lead to destruction.

A few more days with the army stripped him of his last remaining confidence in the cause. King James's support was looking ever more questionable, to the extent that a deeply concerned Lord Feversham recommended they ought to retreat on the grounds that, with the pro-William movement quickly gaining momentum, James's supporters were losing morale. If it should come to a pitched battle, it was not going to be another Sedgemoor, but a contest heavily weighted against them that they would have no chance of winning.

Grafton had already been infuriated with the faint-heartedness of the fleet. Now he was utterly disgusted with the pusillanimity he saw all around them. King James and his closest supporters had completely lost all heart, direction and motivation to fight. His hesitations, lack of resolution to act decisively, and constant vacillation at a time when firm action was needed, showed him that the royal cause was hopeless.

By contrast, the prince of Orange's decisiveness and resolve to act spoke for itself. Churchill and Grafton knew at that point that their sovereign had reached the point of no return, and both changed their allegiance at Axminster on the night of 24 November. On 14 December, the day after Grafton returned to London, he was shot at by a soldier, evidently a Roman Catholic loyalist, near Somerset House. The man's pistol failed to find its mark, but he was immediately identified and shot dead by the duke's men.

It was the decision of the council of general officers to fall back on London, with its inevitable effect of dissolving the loyal elements in the army, which, whatever the value of Churchill's formal plea of conscientious scruples based 'on a high and necessary concern for Religion', finally determined Grafton's conviction that the game was up and that the only chance of securing what the nation desired was to rally to the prince of Orange. The example thus set was soon followed by former devoted adherents of the House of Stuart as the chivalrous Ormond, by Dartmouth himself, and by another of James's nephews, the duke of Northumberland.

King James tersely reprimanded Grafton for his behaviour, telling him, 'You know nothing about religion, you care nothing about it, yet forsooth you must pretend to have a conscience.'

Grafton replied, 'It is true, Sir, I don't pretend to much conscience, but I belong to a party that have a great deal.'[22]

With this, he had made a full declaration of his commitment to the new regime, and set his seal on the change by temporarily leaving William of Orange's camp at Henley to take possession of Tilbury fort with his regiment of foot guards. His next task was to oversee the surrender of the town of Portsmouth, the last stronghold of loyalty to King James. The duke of Berwick, governor of Portsmouth, had been given orders by his father to deliver up the town as soon as any of William of Orange's troops arrived. As they had conceded defeat by this time, it was a peaceful handover that took place without any strife.

Grafton was well-liked and respected by the soldiers under his command, and he had earned a reputation as a conscientious and efficient leader. Moreover, he realised it was a time to be decisive. It was in nobody's interests to allow any kind of drift with regard to crown and government, and he was won over to the conviction that the sense of the country was against any compromise. Too wise and too honourable to oppose or intrigue against the popular wish, he hesitated no longer. Whatever may have been his reasons for showing loyalty to King James, it was now in the national interest to give his unconditional support to the prince and princess of Orange as king and queen of Great Britain and Ireland.

Until the last dying embers of James II's reign, the duke of Northumberland had remained scrupulously loyal. On 11 February 1685, five days after the new king's accession, he had been appointed captain and colonel of the 2nd Troop of Life Guards. A little later, he was forever indebted to King James for having forgiven him after the affair concerning his wife, which had soon been smoothed over. Having put everything behind him, he returned to favour. He commanded the 2nd Troop of Horse Guards in 1687, and he was made a lord of his majesty's bedchamber in November 1688. It was one of the last, perhaps the last, appointment that King James II ever made.

Northumberland's allegiance to his hard-pressed uncle faded as support was draining away from him elsewhere, but he was still in attendance on his majesty on the night of 11 December 1688. It was to his nephew at Whitehall Palace that the king confided his determination to flee the kingdom, asking him to keep it a secret, before he left discreetly by boat at about three o'clock in the morning. As he was planning to leave his kingdom in disguise, he would have a good chance of slipping away undetected. When the door of the royal bedchamber was thrown open at the usual hour of the levee a few hours later, Northumberland came out and told the crowd awaiting his majesty in the antechamber that he had already fled under cover of darkness. It was at that moment that he placed himself at the head of his regiment of guards and declared for the prince of Orange.

4

WILLIAM III, MARY II, AND AFTER

1.

When King James abdicated by deserting his throne and fleeing to France in December 1688, Britain was temporarily without a sovereign. William of Orange therefore took control of the provisional government, and elections were held for a Convention Parliament which assembled on 22 January 1689. In a debate in the House of Lords, the Whigs and Tories argued at length over whether James II was considered to have abdicated or temporarily deserted the throne in some manner, and who then should take the crown.

The Whigs argued that William alone should now be king. A few Radical Whigs argued for a republic, but most favoured a limited monarchy, rather than an absolute one. The Tories, who were largely Stuart loyalists, favoured either the retention of King James II, a regency in his name, or else William's wife, Mary, as queen regnant. Some said that if the sovereign had abdicated and thereby vacated or temporarily deserted the throne, a regency in his name should be established. Grafton was among the forty-nine who voted for such a solution.[1] William cut the debate short by threatening to abandon the country and return to Holland if he was not made king.

On 6 February 1689, the Tory majority in the Lords formally agreed that James II had abdicated and that the crown should pass to Mary as his legitimate heir. The Whig party in the Commons proposed William as king, making him in effect an elected sovereign, and argued that the replacement of one monarch by his heir was not merely justified in the circumstances, but had actually happened. It only remained for parliament to acknowledge the fact and ratify the choice of new sovereign. One week later, William and Mary were formally and jointly offered the crown, their acceptance conditional on the assumption that they would rule according to law and be guided by parliament. They were then proclaimed king and queen.

On 11 April, they were crowned at Westminster Abbey, and the duke of Grafton carried the orb at the ceremony. That summer, he accepted a commission as a private captain in the navy, and he commanded his warship *Grafton* at the Battle of Beachy Head in July, which resulted in a French victory over the combined Anglo-Dutch fleet that the victors failed to exploit. His conduct during the action at sea, where he helped damaged Dutch warships to get clear, brought him a letter of thanks from King William.

Strangely, his unconditional loyalty to the new regime was not immediately repaid in kind. For reasons unknown, possibly jealousy on the part of others who already had the ear of King William, he was soon deprived of his military command without any warning. To his credit, he proved totally magnanimous about this seemingly ungrateful action. In the words of Lord Macaulay, perhaps the first and foremost chronicler of the period, 'though severely mortified, he behaved like a man of sense and spirit; bent on proving that he had been wrongly suspected and animated by an honourable ambition to distinguish himself in his profession'.[2]

As he had already proved earlier in his career, he was a skilled naval commander and one of the most promising that the country had to offer. He no longer needed to stand in the shadow of the earl of Dartmouth, former admiral of the fleet who had remained loyal to King James II to the end and whose attachment to the old regime had led him to be imprisoned in the Tower of London without trial. Such a situation now left Grafton in effect head of the navy by default. He was therefore fittingly granted the king's permission to return to sea in command of his old ship that bore his name. William was well aware of his usefulness to the service, and the fact that he was fully prepared to accept a less senior position—unless he was suddenly to be promoted—proved that he could be fully trusted. An anonymous chronicler of the age recorded in May 1690 that 'The Duke of Grafton was last night four hours in private with the King, and this morning went to view the fleet in harbour.'[3]

It was probably the last occasion on which both men came face to face. After that the king was kept busy with overseeing the preparations for a military expedition to Ireland where the former King James, aided by a coalition of Catholic supporters and French reinforcements, was intent on trying to reclaim his former dominions.

Keen to seize the opportunities ahead of them, Grafton was now focused on activities in another theatre of war, with the French, and impatient with the half-hearted preparations of Captain Torrington to meet the French fleet. William embarked on 20 June, and on the next day Tourville put out to join the fray. He halted William's convoy of six ships which, on the arrival of the expedition at Carrickfergus, were sent to join Torrington at once. Had French naval strategy managed to intercept the communications between England and Ireland, Tourville's fleet might have been used more effectively in the Irish Sea. Tourville found Torrington, lying off the Isle of Wight, so unprepared to meet him that the English admiral spent the first days at sea in withdrawing east to pick up reinforcements. When ordered by William in Ireland to bring the French fleet to action, he had no choice but to risk an encounter, even though his fleet was smaller than that of the enemy. Torrington would emerge from the action that followed with less credit than Grafton, and subsequent events covered the latter with renown as a daring seaman and no mean naval tactician.

Torrington was regarded as a cautious, painstaking, but indecisive commander of whom it was said that his 'greatest ingenuity lay in finding excuses to avoid serious action'.[4] In a battle fought in the English Channel off Beachy Head, on the Sussex coast, on 10 July, he was reluctant to engage the French fleet, perhaps with good reason, as the latter outnumbered the combined Anglo-Dutch naval force. Grafton put up a good fight, fiercely attacking the French ships which had part of the Dutch squadron in their sights. His quick thinking and readiness for action saved several of their ships from destruction.

The battle ended in a French victory, but Grafton was hailed as the hero of the day. Torrington was subsequently court-martialled, charged with having withdrawn, and held back from the action. He blamed defeat on the lack of naval preparations and intelligence, and to the annoyance of King William he was found not guilty. Yet the general view afterwards was that if Grafton had been given supreme command instead, allowed to take the initiative and been permitted to engage the whole fleet, and more quickly, the British and Dutch would certainly have won a great victory.

Grafton's services were recognised by an autograph letter from William, thanking him for his services that day.

Two months later, when a naval expedition was despatched to Ireland with the military forces assigned for the reduction of Cork and Kinsale under Marlborough, Grafton was entrusted with the command of part of the fleet. After returning from the battle, he spent a fortnight at Euston with the duchess, then paid a visit to Evelyn as recorded in his diary of 1 August: 'The Duke of Grafton came to visit me, going to his ship at the mouth of the river on his way to Ireland, where he was slain.'[5] Next he joined Churchill's force, eager for the Irish campaign against the former King James who had just landed there in an effort to regain his crown. After James was defeated at the Battle of the Boyne in July 1690, the Jacobite army retreated to the west of Ireland. King William then sent a force under Churchill to secure the port of Cork on the southern coast.

HMS *Grafton*, somewhat battle-scarred after having been in the thick of action at Beachy Head, was undergoing a complete overhaul and her captain threw himself into the work of preparing her for sea with his customary energy. Once the task was completed, he joined the rest of the fleet at Portsmouth at the end of August. Stormy conditions delayed their departure for nearly three weeks, and they set sail on 17 September, arriving at Crosshaven, at the entrance to Cork Harbour, four days later.

Grafton's enthusiasm and spirit scorned detention on board while there was more active work to be done ashore, and he eagerly put his services as a volunteer at the disposal of the commander-in-chief, a step most welcome to Marlborough, who like King William knew his value as a leader. He was placed at the head of the troops commanding the approaches to the city. Once they were within position and had come within a mile of the town of Cork, they began to mount their cannon and to lay formal siege. Under Marlborough's leadership, outwork after outwork fell in quick succession, and a breach in the main defences was declared practicable.

On 28 September, they mounted an assault on the city. Grafton and several naval officers, inspired by his influence, led the attack, advancing through a waterlogged bog, the Rape Marsh. Despite heavy fire now concentrated on the column, the four English regiments detailed for the charge, up to their shoulders in water, pressed on to the foot of the breach. While 'struggling through the quagmire', Grafton was struck by a musket ball from the ramparts and seriously wounded.[6] He had been hit in the shoulder and sustained a couple of broken ribs. At first everyone was hopeful that he might recover, but his condition soon deteriorated, and he died on 9 October.

Although he had been one of the casualties, the siege was ultimately a success. By taking part in the attack, he had helped to expedite the surrender of the city, once the breach had been reached, with 4,000 men capitulating. Sadly, he had not lived long enough for promotion to come his way. King William had been particularly impressed with his conduct and bravery at the Battle of Beachy Head, and while the younger man was serving in Ireland, he had agreed to appoint him commander in charge of the naval forces on the Irish coast. It would have been a position for which he was well fitted.

After some of his internal organs had been removed and buried in Ballintemple, Cork, to preserve his remains for transport, his body was taken home aboard ship that bore his name, and the vessel docked at London on 1 November. A few days later a funeral service was held for him at Westminster Abbey, and he was then interred in the new Church of St Genevieve at Euston.

The earl of Nottingham, a secretary of state, had been a close friend of Grafton for some years. On his death, he opined that the duke was 'a very gallant man, and extremely beloved by the seamen, with whom he was very familiar and often joined them in their rough sports, and had he lived, would have deserved to have been Lord Admiral'.[7]

His name would live on in the land in which he had fallen. Grafton Alley, Cork, close to where he was shot, was named after him. Grafton Street, one of the main streets in the commercial sector of Dublin, was named in honour of him and the family. There is some doubt as to whether it was after the first duke or his son, the second, who owned land in the countryside which later became part of the city.

He was succeeded as duke by his son, Charles Fitzroy, at the time a boy of almost seven. Within a few years, he had entered royal service. In March 1698, at the age of fourteen, he was appointed master of the horse to William, duke of Gloucester, the only surviving child of William's sister-in-law and heir, Anne. Meanwhile in October 1697, the widowed duchess had married Sir Thomas Hanmer, who later became Speaker of the House of Commons and was considered one of the foremost Shakespeare authorities of his day. She died on 7 February 1723.

*****

Although the duke of Northumberland had been loyal to King James II almost until the final moment, he refrained from joining him on his ignominious journey across the Channel into exile. Instead, he immediately gave his allegiance to William and Mary, and sat in the Lords during the Convention Parliament. Although he was asked to relinquish his command of the Horse Guards to James Butler, 2nd duke of Ormond, he did not find himself out of favour during the new reign. He was comfortably provided for, being given a pension of £3,000 a year from the excise to add to the £2,350 he already received from the Post Office. A few years later, he was appointed lord lieutenant of Surrey, constable of Windsor Castle and Park, and ranger of Windsor Forest.

On the death of King William III (Queen Mary having died of smallpox in 1694) and the accession of Queen Anne in 1702, less than five months after the death of the exiled James II in France, the duke of Northumberland retained his largely ceremonial posts and also became keeper of Hampton Court Palace. Although he retained a great interest in military matters, there is some doubt as to whether he fought during the War of the Spanish Succession or not. He was appointed colonel of the Royal Horse Guards on 13 March 1703 on the death of Aubrey de Vere, 20th earl of Oxford, and promoted to major-general on 27 April 1708. When Ormond became captain-general in January 1712, he was given back his old posts as captain and colonel of the 2nd Life Guards. To add to his other posts, he was made lord lieutenant of Berkshire later that year and became a privy councillor in August 1713.

As a fervent Tory, Northumberland would find himself out of favour with the crown after the passing of the last Stuart monarch. The Tories had always been loyal first and foremost to the Stuart line, and in particular 'The Old Pretender', many of them secretly believing him to be the rightful heir to his childless half-sisters and therefore their king. Of Queen Anne's seventeen pregnancies (all of which took place before she ascended the throne in 1702), only five had resulted in live births. Out of these, two daughters lived to twenty months and eight months respectively, and a son, William, duke of Gloucester, died just after his eleventh birthday.

This left his mother as the only individual remaining in the Protestant line of succession established by the Bill of Rights in 1689. As this legislation expressly forbade a Catholic to ascend the British throne, in 1701 an Act of Settlement was passed by parliament recognising Electress

Sophia of Hanover, a Protestant cousin of Charles II (whose wife it was once thought she might become) and James II, and her issue as heirs to the throne. Although thirty-four years older, Sophia was in considerably more robust health than her second cousin, Anne, and had she outlived her she would have succeeded as queen regnant—at the age of eighty-three. Anne died in August 1714, having outlived her by seven weeks, and Sophia's son, now elector of Hanover, ascended the British throne as King George I. The Whigs had just regained control of the government and were seen as more friendly to the incoming Hanoverian dynasty. Somewhat tainted on account of his Tory associations, Northumberland lost his various posts at Windsor, his lieutenancies, and his place on the Privy Council.

*****

Cardell Goodman, who had been the countess of Castlemaine's partner for a short time, was a fervent Jacobite. In 1696, he was implicated in a plot to assassinate King William III and was imprisoned but offered a free pardon to give evidence against Sir John Fenwick, the leading conspirator. Shunned by his partners in crime for turning informer, he fled to France and died soon afterwards.

The earl of Castlemaine, the much-cuckolded husband and model of dignified silence, from whom his wife had never been divorced in spite of all the heartache she had caused him, died in 1705. In his last will and testament, dated 30 November 1696, he had nominated two trustees. One was a close friend and adviser, rather than family. The other was 'my Lady Ann, now Countess of Sussex', his eldest 'daughter', who was left his property in the Savoy and his leaseholds in Monmouthshire, as well as his plate, jewels, and other possessions.

Legally free at last, Barbara married Major-General Robert Fielding, a fortune-hunter whom she discovered had married another woman two weeks earlier, a Mary Wadsworth, mistakenly believing that she was an heiress. She had him prosecuted for bigamy, cancelled an allowance she had undertaken to pay him, and then had to apply to the magistrates for protection from his 'barbarous ill-treatment' of her. Aged sixty-eight, her eventful life came to an end on 9 October 1709 at her home, Walpole House in Chiswick Mall, after suffering from congestive heart failure.

Her daughter, Anne, countess of Sussex, was a Roman Catholic, and it was not her brazen infidelity (which the earl apparently learnt to put up with) but instead religious differences that would prove the final undoing between wife and husband, a staunch Protestant. They parted company at around the time of the Glorious Revolution in 1688, when she went to the former James II's court St Germain-en-Laye, taking both their daughters with her, and became a lady-in-waiting to the former Queen Mary. The earl, who had been a gentleman of the bedchamber, found himself impoverished after years of extravagance, especially gambling, and litigation, and had to sell Herstmonceux. He spent his last years at Chevening and died in 1715. His widow died on 16 May 1722 and was buried at Linsted, Kent.

*****

In accordance with the plans made several years earlier, Charles, duke of Southampton, eldest son of the countess of Castlemaine, had married Mary Wood in 1679, but she died of smallpox on 15 November 1680. His inheritance of her estate was challenged by the Wood family, and after lengthy litigation, the House of Lords decided in favour of Southampton in 1692. In 1694, he married Anne, a daughter of Sir William Poultney, of Misterton, Leicestershire, and they had six children.

For the next few years, he lived quietly, out of the public eye. He took almost no interest in politics, although he was named as a participant in a Jacobite conspiracy in 1691. William Fuller was an opportunist who claimed to be a distant relative of William Herbert, 1st marquis of Powis. Most, if not all, of the information handed down to posterity about his life and career is based on his word alone and has to be regarded as highly suspect, if not sheer fantasy. Through this apparent connection he came to the attention of Queen Mary in 1688, shortly before the birth of James Edward Stuart. By the end of the year, the former King James, Queen Mary, and their baby son were on their way to exile in France, with Fuller travelling as part of the company as a page to Lady Powis, who had been appointed governess to Prince James Edward. Within a few months, he claimed, he was carrying secret messages between the former king's court at St Germain-en-Laye and his Catholic supporters in England, still eager for a restoration.

On one such visit in 1689, his behaviour aroused suspicion and he was arrested. When brought before King William III, he undertook to continue passing messages from the Jacobites, working as a double agent on the grounds that the new king would be able to afford to pay him better. This came to an end when his associate, Matthew Crone, was arrested and convicted, and Fuller was exposed as an informant of little value at best and an outright charlatan at worst. Such sums as he had been given for his highly dubious work were discontinued at once. At around this time, he made the acquaintance of or at least had some connection with Titus Oates, who knew more than a little about spreading news about bogus plots. Deeply in debt and thrown into jail, he thought he found his financial salvation in contacting the archbishop of Canterbury, John Tillotson, and the earl of Portland, one of King William's oldest friends and most trusted advisers. He wrote to them saying he had firm evidence of a Jacobite plot in high places.

Among those he named were the dukes of Southampton and Northumberland. He had evidently not learnt from Oates that naming innocent people in high places was a waste of time, if not worse, if he had no evidence to back up such allegations—which he plainly had not. When Tillotson and Portland both ignored his correspondence, he took his allegations to parliament, and he was summoned to appear before the bar of the Commons. For his pains, he was awarded a lump sum and a weekly allowance. Every time he was challenged to produce his evidence, he offered excuses why he could not, either saying that his papers were detained elsewhere or else pleading inability to appear through ill-health. At length, the Commons saw through his tissue of lies, and in February 1692, a motion was passed declaring him a 'notorious Impostor, a Cheat, and a false Accuser'. He was tried and convicted in November, sentenced to stand in the pillory, and then sent back to jail.

In 1697, Southampton was awarded a pension of £1,000 *per annum* on the proceeds of the lotteries. Although he took little if any part in Lords debates, he joined the protest against the abandonment of the amendments to the Irish Forfeitures and Land Tax Bill in 1700. This was a contentious measure that had left Tories and Whigs strongly divided, relating to the land settlement arising from William III's victory in Ireland during what became known as the War of the Two Kings in the first two years of his reign.

There had been assurances that estates forfeited by James's supporters would be sold with monies raised used to offset the costs of a successful campaign and returned to the national exchequer, but instead William awarded much of the land to his military commanders and personal favourites after the end of the conflict. Members of parliament thought this amounted to royal reneging on what had been regarded as a firm undertaking to the nation, and sought to overturn his policy. The bill, also sometimes referred to by the shorter name of the Act of Resumption, cancelled most of the king's decisions on redistributing the estates, and proposed vesting all identifiably forfeited property in a thirteen-man board of trustees. Some members voted to halt these amendments, a move that resulted in a degree of compromise during the passage of the legislation.

Apart from this rare venture into the political waters, Southampton lived quietly out of the public eye. Like his father before him, he took a great interest in the theatre, and was happy to extend his patronage to companies of actors. When his mother died in 1709, he succeeded to the barony of Nonsuch and Surrey, and the earldom of Southampton. He also took her title, becoming 2nd duke of Cleveland by a special remainder in the grant of the dukedom that set aside his illegitimacy, and took his seat in the House of Lords on 14 January 1710.

Occasional religious controversies would demonstrate how divided the half-brothers could be. A fearless outspoken Fellow of Magdalen College, Oxford, Dr Henry Sacheverell, made a name for himself through preaching sermons and issuing pamphlets in which his main targets were Whigs and moderate Tories. In one address, which he delivered before the lord mayor and aldermen of London in November 1709, he spoke critically of the Whig minister Sidney Godolphin, and of his hostility to the principles of the Glorious Revolution some twenty years earlier. Sacheverell was tried for sedition by the House of Lords, and a group of Londoners staged riots in sympathy with him. Nevertheless, he was convicted in March 1710 and suspended from preaching for three years.

Southampton was among those who voted in favour of declaring him guilty. His wife was a defender of the controversial cleric, and it was believed that she had advised his brother, the strongly Tory duke of Northumberland, to escort him to the House of Lords to ensure that he voted against the measure, but his half-brother, Richmond, smuggled him out of his house in order to persuade Southampton to vote for Sacheverell's guilt.

The rest of Southampton's life passed uneventfully. He died at his home in St James's Square, Westminster, on 9 September 1730 and was buried at Westminster Abbey. Within two years of his death, his estates were believed to be worth 'more than £100,000 a year'. His widow married landscape gardener Philip Southcote on 3 February 1732 and died on 20 February 1746. Her first husband was succeeded as duke by their eldest son, William Fitzroy, who died without issue, when all his titles became extinct. There were two other sons, Charles and Henry Fitzroy, and three daughters, Grace (later countess of Darlington), Anne, and Barbara.

*****

The earl and countess of Lichfield, the latter being the countess of Castlemaine's second daughter, had eighteen children. Several of them died either in infancy, or very soon after attaining maturity. Two of their three sons subsequently succeeded to the earldom, George, who was his father's eldest surviving son, and in turn followed by his son. The latter died without issue and was therefore succeeded by his childless uncle, Robert, the last of the line. Charlotte died on 17 February 1718, seventeen months after her husband.

*****

George, duke of Northumberland, the countess of Castlemaine's youngest son, continued to serve his sovereigns in a military capacity as well as in the royal household. He was made constable of Windsor Castle and lord lieutenant of Surrey in 1701, and the latter post of Berkshire in 1712. He succeeded the earl of Oxford as colonel of the Royal Regiment of Horse in March 1703, and on 10 January 1710, he obtained the rank of lieutenant-general. He was sworn of the Privy Council on 7 April 1713 and was also chief butler of England.

Although his marriage to Catherine Wheatley had been followed by some strange adventures involving the duke of Grafton, he never had any cause to regret what had seemed a lowly marriage for the son of a king. They enjoyed a peaceful married life of nearly thirty years, untainted by any further controversy. The duchess died on 25 May 1714, and on 10 March 1715, he married Mary Dutton. He died at his Epsom home on 28 June 1716, leaving no issue by either wife, and was buried in Westminster Abbey on 11 July. His widow died at Frogmore, his house in Windsor Great Park, on 27 August 1738. He left no children by either of his wives, and with his death the title became extinct. Contemporaries apparently found him a pleasant if unexceptional character, according to the spy John Macky, who judged him to be 'a man of honour, nice in paying his debts, and living well with his neighbours in the country: does not much care for the conversation of men of quality and business; is a tall black man, like his father the King'.[8]

*****

Like his mother, Nell Gwyn, the young duke of St Albans was determined to resist King James II's pressure to make him convert to Catholicism. When she died in 1687, he went to the continent, ostensibly to Hungary to join the Roman Catholic Church, in accordance with his uncle's requirement. Once he was out of England, he had other priorities. Joining the army there, he became a colonel in the 8th Regiment of Horse, serving under Leopold I, Holy Roman emperor. He was one of the officers present at the siege of Belgrade in September 1688, at which imperial Habsburg troops under the command of Maximilian II Emanuel, elector of Bavaria, captured the city from the Ottoman Empire during the Great Turkish War fought between 1683 and 1699.

His mission accomplished, he then went to the Dutch Republic where he became one of William of Orange's most fervent supporters in his mission to invade England and become king. His loyalty was rewarded, and during the next few years, he fought in the imperial army, commanded a horse regiment, and served under William III in Flanders several times. His new sovereign bestowed on him various gifts, such as a pension of £2,000 from the crown, and a set of spotted coach horses after his role in the signing of the Treaty of Ryswick in 1697, which brought to an end the nine years of conflict between France on one side and a coalition of England, the Dutch Republic, and the Holy Roman Empire. He was also made captain of the Gentlemen Pensioners, and a few years later gentleman of the bedchamber. In 1705, he received a further grant of £800 per year from the parliament of Ireland.

In April 1694, he had married Lady Diana De Vere, eldest daughter and co-heir to the twentieth and last earl of Oxford, and they had twelve children. Because of his Whig sympathies he was regarded with some suspicion by Queen Anne, but he was restored to favour at the accession of King George I, who liked him and in 1718 made him a Knight of the Garter. By this time, the duchess had already been appointed lady of the bedchamber to Caroline, princess of Wales.

The duke died at Bath in 1726, two days after his fifty-sixth birthday, and he was buried in Westminster Abbey; his eldest son succeeded to the title. John Macky noted that he was 'a gentleman every way *de bon naturel*, well-bred, doth not love business; is well affected to the constitution of his country. He is of a black complexion, not so tall as the Duke of Northumberland, yet very like King Charles.'[9]

The duke of Richmond returned to France when William became king, and despite having been treated so coldly, he still pledged his loyalty to the uncle who still seemed intent on reclaiming the crown he had just forfeited. He still hankered after a career in the army and was sure that the military campaign in Ireland would provide a perfect opportunity, but James initially told him that at sixteen years of age he was too young and too small. Perhaps it was just as well, for the enterprise was a total failure, but his persistence was rewarded. He got on very well with Louis XIV, who often took him out wolf hunting. The king was so impressed with him that he made him an officer in the campaign against a Dutch attack on Valcourt in the Spanish Netherlands in August 1689 during the Nine Years' War, fought between France and the Grand Alliance, a coalition including the Dutch Republic, the Holy Roman Empire, England, Spain, and Savoy.

John Churchill, now earl of Marlborough, was in charge of defending the town. Richmond was keen to do his duty in any way possible. Appointed *aide-de-camp* to Philippe, duc d'Orleans, nephew of King Louis (and son of 'Minette', the sister of Charles II and James II), he acquitted himself well though the battle ended in heavy defeat for the French army, who lost over 2,000 men while their enemies' casualties were about a third of the number. In September 1690, the king appointed him commander of the Royal Horse Regiment. Although he had declared his allegiance to the Catholic faith, he was not in any of the regiments that accompanied the former King James to Ireland in the effort to reclaim his crown by force of arms. However, he was sent to the Low Countries for a time, and he wrote to his mother that he was sure she would be very proud of his efforts.

Meanwhile, the duchess of Portsmouth was living as ever beyond her means. King William could hardly be expected to make provision for her, especially as it was considered that she had already taken an astonishing amount of money from England with her and was not deserving of any more. In 1689, King Louis XIV gave her an extra annual allowance of £12,000, and the duke of Richmond and his family a further £20,000. As he had no obligation to do so, this was generous indeed. Her next couple of years were similarly unhappy, for in 1690 she lost her father, and soon afterwards a fire at Whitehall destroyed her apartment and the precious furniture she had left there in the event of her returning to live in London.

As for her son, he seemed restless, discontented, longing to prove himself at something. Perhaps he considered himself unfulfilled and that as the son of a king, even though he might be illegitimate, he expected rather more from King Louis than merely being granted commands in the French army. Hoping that the grass would be greener on the other side, and sure that he would be promoted to a far higher rank and be paid much better in England, he turned his back on France. It was a surprise to his mother and to King Louis when he suddenly decided without telling them that he wanted to return to service in the land of his birth. After going back briefly to Paris, he left secretly for England, travelling incognito via Switzerland and Germany. His mother strongly suspected that he had stolen some of his mother's jewels in order to provide money for his journey.

She told King Louis XIV that she was astonished by her son's folly, that she believed he had gone in search of a place at the court of King William III, and she totally despaired of him. Angered at his abrupt departure after all he had done recently for the young man, King Louis reduced the family pension to 12,000 *livres* and it reverted to the duchess of Portsmouth, thus cutting her son off from French support. She was equally indignant at his behaviour, and from then on relations between them were never the same again.

On 8 January 1692, he married Anne Brudenell, widow of Henry, Baron Belasyse, and daughter of Francis, Baron Brudenell. He renounced his Catholicism at a ceremony at Lambeth Palace in May 1692, returned to the Anglican Communion, and as he had planned, made his peace with William III. In November 1693, he took his seat in the House of Lords, and the following year he was made lord high admiral of Scotland. He was also made grandmaster of the Freemasons of England in 1696.

Richmond's move back to England and subsequent appointments under William III had fulfilled his expectations that he could live more comfortably than before. In 1697, he purchased the country estate of Goodwood, near Chichester, Sussex. For the rest of the reign, he served as an *aide-de-camp* in Flanders. In spite of this, he was regarded as a turncoat, and in 1696, he was suspected of complicity in ongoing Jacobite conspiracies. It was thought that he was still a devout papist at heart and wanted a Catholic king back on the throne. William III suspected that he still harboured Jacobite sympathies and was maintaining contact with the leading advocates of a restoration of the king whose abdication had been a result of his invasion in 1688. For a short period, he was obliged to leave England, but was allowed to return in January 1697. Any doubts about his unconditional loyalty cannot have run deep, as he had become an *aide-de-camp* to the new sovereign and for most of the time seemed faithful enough to the new regime. His main fault was that he seemed to be weak, easily led but above all preferred to lead a quiet life and be left alone.

Although she remained in France, the duchess of Portsmouth continued to live beyond her means. Now that her son and his family had settled contentedly in Sussex, and as he appeared to be living the life of a good loyal subject to King William, there was nothing to be lost and perhaps something to be gained in laying her financial worries before the sovereign. She arrived at Dover in August 1698 and Richmond met her there. Any lingering grievances and disputes between them had long since been forgiven and forgotten, and it was a happy reunion. Invited to stay at their home in Sussex, she was very pleased to meet her granddaughter, four-year-old Louisa, born in December 1694, for the first time. In September, she presented a petition to the king humbly asking for the grant of a pension of £8,000. The following month, it was noticed by members of the court that she attended a service at St James's Church, and it was rumoured that she had followed her son's example and joined the Anglican Church. This appears to have been ill-founded, and in February 1699, she returned to France, having obtained a pension of only £1,000.

Now that the duke of Richmond was enjoying a peaceful life on his countryside, before long he developed a passion for cricket. Thought to have originated as a children's game during Saxon or Norman times, by the early seventeenth century, it was increasingly played by adults, and began to flourish after the Restoration, though usually regarded as a gambling sport indulged in by the wealthy, and usually for high stakes. The duke was an early patron of the game; regarded as one of the pioneer professional sportsmen, his enthusiasm and encouragement of others did much to develop it in Sussex. Records suggest that he was involved with the earliest known 'great match', which took place in the 1697 summer season and was probably the first to be reported by the English press. The *Foreign Post noted:* 'The middle of last week a great match at cricket was played in Sussex; there were eleven of a side, and they played for fifty guineas apiece.'[10] Such remuneration and the fact that it was an eleven-a-side contest suggests that the organisers had gone to some effort to choose two strong and well-balanced teams. No other details were given, but the report of what may have been an inter-county match suggested that cricket, played for high stakes, was being taken seriously. He later sponsored a team in the 1702 season against an Arundel side. It was a passion that he passed down to his son, Charles, the 2nd duke, who inherited his interest and became the patron of both cricket teams in his home county and Slindon Cricket Club, near Chichester.

The duke and duchess of Richmond had two more children. Charles was born in 1701 and Anne in 1703. The duke had remained in favour at court at the accession of Queen Anne in 1702, and he played a minor ceremonial role at her coronation at Westminster Abbey in April, when he carried the sceptre with the dove. The queen attended the christening of little Anne and presented the family with 200 ounces of gilt plate to mark the occasion. The duchess of Portsmouth was delighted with the growing family, and later wrote very affectionate letters to young Charles.

In October 1702, Frances, dowager duchess of Richmond, passed away. She was best remembered for refusing to become a mistress of King Charles II and also, according to some (but disputed by others), for modelling the image of Britannia as it appeared on British coinage from 1672 onwards. Having been widowed at an early age, she never remarried and left no children, so the ownership of the Lennox estates passed to Duke Charles. He sold them at once, adding handsomely to his fortune from the revenue as a result but retaining his peerage. During the reigns of Queen Anne and George I, he was made a lord of the bedchamber and privy councillor. Despite these favours, some of the others at court still thought his allegiance and politics remained changeable according to circumstances. Regarded as a notorious opportunist with an uncanny knack of being on the winning side, he altered his religious beliefs and political alliances to suit his interests and ambitions, and his ever-changing stance on political and religious issues meant he was never truly considered a faithful or capable servant to any particular cause.

In May 1712, he returned briefly to Paris for no apparent reason, staying about a year. King George I appointed him gentleman of the bedchamber on 16 October 1714. Despite his wealth, he did not seem to render any assistance to his mother or to have taken any interest in the duchy of Aubigny. His son, Charles, married Sarah Cadogan in December 1719, so he could settle a gambling debt between their parents. The marriage was arranged by both fathers in order to cancel a gambling debt incurred by Lord Cadogan. Dowry and debt were due to a sum won by her father in play against his father. Despite what looked like a very calculated arrangement, it proved to be a happy union, and through their twelve children, they secured the lineage of the Richmond and Lennox family. Sarah was appointed a lady of the bedchamber to Caroline, princess of Wales, and remained in the post when she became queen consort in 1727.

Louisa, Richmond's first child, married James, 3rd earl of Berkeley, in February 1711. She was not well-liked among her contemporaries, and at the time of her wedding, writer Jonathan Swift, also renowned as a satirist and cleric, described her as 'ill-natured, covetous, vicious and proud in extremes'. They had two children, Augustus and Elizabeth. In 1714, she was appointed a lady of the bedchamber to Caroline, princess of Wales, but in January 1716, she succumbed to smallpox, aged thirty-one. Her younger sister, Anne, the second daughter, married Willem van Keppel, 2nd earl of Albemarle. She was also a lady of the bedchamber to Queen Caroline and became a great favourite of King George II. He paid her an annual pension of £1,500 *per annum* when Albemarle died in 1754, which was fortuitous as he was renowned for being a spendthrift who left his family deeply in debt.

As for the 1st duke of Richmond, nineteenth-century French historian Henri Forneron was particularly scathing in his verdict on a man in whom he found few if any redeeming qualities:

> The young Duke of Richmond entered the Catholic Church, but was not for that the less corrupt and vicious. He relapsed to Anglican Protestantism, or rather lived and died a godless life, and was to its end plunged in drunkenness and debauchery. From being one of the handsomest young men in England he became the most hideous old rake.[11]

Even one of his descendants, the 8th duke, who wrote a biography of the 2nd duke early in the twentieth century, had to admit that there was little to be said about him that put him in a good light.

> [While he filled a few public offices] yet his unfortunate propensity for being everything by turns and nothing long (and this in matters religious as well as political) effectually militated against any chance of his name being emblazoned upon the scroll of Fame. A few tattered and barely decipherable letters lie before me as I write; they are all that is left of his private or family correspondence, and as I read over once again the letters of Duchess Anne, his wife, hurriedly penned (for they bear no date) to Louise de Keroualle (at her Chateau of Aubigny), who was making anxious inquiries as to the truth of sundry evil reports that had come to her ears about her son, one cannot help feeling that both ladies had good cause to be worried.[12]

It was not politics or religion that would be the cause of his downfall or rather premature demise; self-indulgence was his ruin. He and his half-brother, Charles, duke of St Albans, the surviving son of Nell Gwyn and King Charles, were married men with wives and children, but that never stopped them from being regular clients of a well-known London prostitute, Sally Pridden, also known as Sally Salisbury. She prided herself on providing services mostly to wealthy aristocratic patrons, who were also said to include the prince of Wales, later King George II, among others. There was always a handsome sum to be earned from assignations with the sons of kings and their deep pockets. Her career came to an inglorious end when she was charged with stabbing and wounding one of her customers, John Finch, son of the earl of Nottingham, for which she was imprisoned in Newgate and died a few months later from syphilis.

By another mistress, Jacqueline de Mézières, the duke of Richmond had a daughter, Renée Lennox. She carried on something of a family tradition by becoming the mistress of Charles Beauclerk, the 2nd duke of St Albans and a grandson of King Charles II and Nell Gwyn, by whom the duke of St Albans had a daughter, Diane. Yet probably for want of anything better to do with his time, a debauched lifestyle soon got the better of Richmond. By his late forties, a combination of heavy drinking and probably venereal disease had left him, in his loyal but despairing wife's words, 'broke and decayed'.

In fact, she passed away first, dying at Goodwood in December 1722, and her widower followed her on 27 May 1723. When he was told of the news, diarist and antiquarian Thomas Hearne recalled a conversation with him in Oxford some years before, and was left with the impression of 'a man of very little understanding, and though the son of so great a King as Charles II, was a man that struck in with every thing that was whiggish and opposite to true monarchical principles'.[13] Jonathan Swift was even more dismissive, calling him 'a shallow coxcomb'. A more charitable note was struck by John Macky, who found him 'good-natured to a fault, very well bred, with many valuable things in him; was an enemy to business, very credulous, well shaped, black complexion, much like King Charles'.[14] He was buried at Westminster Abbey in the Richmond Chapel, built by King Henry VII, formerly earl of Richmond. His body was reinterred in the Lady Chapel at Chichester Cathedral in August 1750.

Though she had not seen or had any contact with him for several years, the countess of Portsmouth sincerely mourned her only child in a letter to her grandson:

> I am sure that you cannot doubt my being acutely distressed at the death of your Father, and that I feel the emotion of a tender mother such as I have always been to him, although I suffered from his lack of response. But it is 'my son' that I have lost, a fact that makes it impossible for me to restrain very bitter tears. And yet, the Lord God who is always good, leaves me one consolation in you, of whom I have always every reason to be satisfied, for I dare flatter myself, my dear boy, that you have a sincere tenderness and affection for a grandmother that has the most lifelong devotion for you; and I shall not consider myself so unhappy, my dear Lord, if you are just a little bit sensible of it.[15]

As he predeceased his mother by eleven years, he never held the French dukedom, and the heir on her death in 1734 would be his son, Charles, who had always been close to his grandmother and visited her at her estates in Aubigny, in addition to the dukedoms of Richmond and Lennox. The younger Charles had become MP for Chichester in 1722, but he gave up his seat on succeeding to the dukedom. He inherited not only his father's title, but also his passion for cricket, and he captained his own team.

When King George II ascended the throne in 1727, Charles was appointed lord of the bedchamber, and eight years later master of the horse. He was well-respected at court, though Queen Caroline took a dislike to him. She found him 'so half witted, so bizarre, and so grandseigneur, and so mulish, that he is as troublesome from meaning well and comprehending so ill, as if he meant as ill as he comprehends'.[16] Her view was not shared by Lord Hervey, a vice-chamberlain in the royal household, who greatly admired him:

> There never lived a man of more amiable composition; he was kindly, benevolent, generous, honourable, and thoroughly noble in his way of acting, talking and thinking; he had constant spirits, was very entertaining, and had a great deal of knowledge, though, not having had a school education, he was a long while reckoned ignorant by the generality of the world, who are as apt to call every man a blockhead that does not understand Latin and Greek, as they are to think many of those no blockheads who understand nothing else.[17]

In 1735, the 2nd duke was one of the founding governors of the Foundling Hospital in London, a charity dedicated to saving abandoned children in the city. He regularly attended committee meetings, and with the duchess took part in the baptism and naming of the first children to be accepted by the hospital in March 1741. Although he did not have an active military career, he became a lieutenant-general and served under George, duke of Cumberland, who led the royal orces against the Jacobite Rising in 1745. In 1750, he fell ill with an inflammation of the bladder, died in August, aged forty-nine, and was buried in Chichester Cathedral at the same time as his father's body was reinterred there. His wife never got over his death and died less than a year later.

*****

The youngest of the countess of Castlemaine's six daughters led a quiet life far away from the British Court. In November 1689, Lady Barbara Fitzroy, then aged seventeen, became a novice at the Convent of the English Benedictines in Pontoise, Normandy. She professed her vows of poverty, chastity, and obedience in April 1691 and took the name Benedicta. In spite of this, she was alleged to have had an affair with James, the duke of Hamilton, and given birth to his son, Charles, who was brought up by the countess of Castlemaine and later became the count of Arran as the earl's parents strongly disapproved of his liaison. The same legend also says that the countess of Castlemaine doted on her hapless grandson but disowned her daughter, but the dates of her becoming a nun tend to disprove the story.[18]

A lack of certain facts about so many of the family has led to her sometimes being confused with her sister, Cecilia, who was not only also a nun but is sometimes thought to have been the mother of Charles, later count of Arran. Benedicta left the Benedictines in August 1721 to take up a new post as prioress of the Royal Priory of St Nicolas, where she remained until her death in 1737.

*****

In December 1686, almost two years after King Charles's death, Moll Davis married French musician and composer James Paisible, a recorder virtuoso who had been working in London for several years and become a member of James II's Private Musick, the select organisation of vocal and instrumental ensembles employed by the royal family. They both accompanied the king to France after he abdicated in 1688 and was exiled at St Germain-en-Laye. At around this time, they found it necessary to resort to legal action in order to claim funds that Moll was owed, probably from the pension that had been awarded to her by King Charles. They were successful and returned to London in 1693, where Paisible resumed his musical services to the court by becoming a composer to Prince George of Denmark. Moll died in 1708 and her widower in 1721.

Her daughter, Lady Mary, had been surrounded throughout her childhood by the cream of Restoration high society. As she became used to the company of dramatists, artists, poets, and those of a similar calling, it was not surprising that she soon followed in her mother's footsteps. She began acting at a young age, and took part in performances at court, among them singing the part of Cupid alongside her mother, starring as Venus, in Shakespeare's *Venus and Adonis*.

On 18 August 1687, she married Viscount Edward Radcliffe, who was born on 9 December 1655 and succeeded his father on his death in 1697 as 2nd earl of Derwentwater. They had three sons, James, Charles, and Francis, and a daughter, Mary. Francis died suddenly in his early twenties. Lady Mary separated from her husband in 1700, reportedly because of religious differences as she had no desire to convert to Roman Catholicism. There were also rumours that her infidelity caused him much unhappiness, though this seems to have been a secondary reason. They never divorced, and he died on 29 April 1705.

She had been living with Henry Graham, MP for Westmorland, and she married him on 23 May, having been a widow for less than a month. Graham had previously held office in the household of Prince George of Denmark, but the moral code at court had become a little more straitlaced in recent years. Their living in sin was frowned on, and soon after their wedding he was dismissed from his position. His term of disgrace did not last long, for he died on 7 January 1707, less than two years later. Seven months into her second widowhood, on 26 August that year she took as her third husband Major James Rooke. All that is known of her last years is that she died in Paris on 5 November 1726, aged fifty-three. Rooke subsequently remarried and died in 1773.

The Radcliffe family was evidently divided strongly on religious lines. James, who succeeded his father as 3rd earl of Derwentwater, and Charles were both fervent Jacobites as well as Roman Catholics. When James Stuart, son of King James II, tried to regain the throne for the Stuart dynasty in the rising of 1715, one year after the accession of King George I and the beginning of the Hanoverian dynasty, the brothers joined them. It ended with a defeat for the Stuart cause at the Battle of Preston in November, when they were captured, tried for treason, and sentenced to death. Charles escaped from captivity and fled to France. Petitions to King George to show clemency and release James were to no avail, and he was beheaded. From abroad, Charles remained active on behalf of the cause. A second rebellion in 1745 under James Stuart's son and heir, also named Charles, was likewise defeated by the royal forces under King George II. Charles Radcliffe was captured again and beheaded in December 1746.

*****

The duchess of Portsmouth spent most of her last years on the estates at her beloved Aubigny. She made several short visits to England, the final one probably being in October 1714 when she attended the coronation of George I. This was remarked upon by Catherine Sedley, countess of Dorchester, a mistress of James II, when they met Elizabeth Hamilton, countess of Orkney, who had briefly played a similar role during the reign of William III. Between them, 'we three whores' had each been in turn the *maitresse en titre* for successive kings of Britain over nearly four decades.

Louise's pensions and a grant on the Irish revenue given her by Charles II were lost either in the reign of James II or at the Revolution of 1688. If King James had respected his brother's dying wishes, he had been powerless to keep his throne long enough to ensure her a comfortable old age.

Not one to break the habit of a lifetime, she continued to live beyond her means and was almost constantly in debt. King Louis XIV, and after his death in 1715, the regent, Philippe II, duc d'Orleans, gave her a pension and protected her against her creditors. The longest-lived of the mothers of King Charles's children, she died in Paris on 14 November 1734, aged eighty-five. The disease with which he had inadvertently infected her may have put an end to her childbearing days, but certainly did not shorten her life. If the two youngest children of the countess of Castlemaine were fathered by men other than King Charles II, as seems probable, the duchess of Portsmouth outlived all of his offspring.

APPENDIX I

THE DESCENDANTS

Seven of King Charles II's mistresses had at least one child by him. The third, Catherine Pegge, is the one about whose life least is known, beyond the fact that she later married and had a daughter by her husband. Of the two children born to her and the king, their son, Charles Fitzcharles, earl of Plymouth, married but died at the age of twenty-three of dysentery while serving with the army at Tangier, leaving no issue. All that is known of their daughter, Catherine, is that she either died in childhood or became a nun at Dunkirk, therefore leaving no descendants.

As for the remaining six, Lucy Barlow was the first. Her son, James, duke of Monmouth, and his wife, Anne, 1st duchess of Buccleuch, had six children, but two sons and two daughters died in infancy and only two sons lived to maturity. The elder, also called James, became earl of Dalkeith and through his mother (who was duchess of Buccleuch in her own right) duke of Buccleuch. The younger, Henry, became earl of Deloraine. James died of natural causes (apoplexy) at the age of thirty, and his eldest son, Francis, then aged ten, immediately became earl of Dalkeith. Anne, duchess of Monmouth and Dalkeith, whose first title was not affected by her husband's attainder, outlived her son by twenty-six years, surviving until 1732. On her death, her grandson became the 2nd duke of Buccleuch, and both titles (plus others in the Scottish peerage) have subsequently been used by the eldest son to the present day, Buccleuch being the primary title. The duke of Monmouth had forfeited his title by his attainder in 1685, but his subsidiary titles, earl of Doncaster and Baron Scott of Tindale, were restored by King George II in 1743 to his grandson, Francis Scott, 2nd duke of Buccleuch, eight years before his death.

Elizabeth Killigrew's daughter by the then-Prince Charles, Charlotte, married twice. Her first husband, James Howard, a playwright, died at the age of nineteen. Their daughter, Stuarta, became a lady-in-waiting to Queen Mary II and died unmarried in 1706. Charlotte married her second husband, William Paston, who became 2nd Viscount Yarmouth in 1683. He had no surviving male issue, and the titles became extinct on his death in 1732.

It is generally accepted that Barbara Villiers had five children by Charles II. She had seven altogether, but the two youngest were not acknowledged by the king and are believed to have been fathered by Henry Jermyn and by John Churchill, later duke of Marlborough, respectively. The eldest son, Charles, was created duke of Southampton in 1675 and on his mother's death in 1709 also inherited her title of duke of Cleveland. His first marriage was childless, but his second produced six sons. On his death in 1730, the titles passed to his son, William, who died without issue in 1774 and they became briefly extinct.

The dukedom of Southampton was created again in 1781 and one of the heirs was another Charles Fitzroy, Baron Southampton, a descendant of a brother of the 1st duke of Southampton and also the great-great-grandson through an illegitimate line of King Charles II and the duchess of Cleveland. The second son, Henry, created duke of Grafton in 1675, had one son who succeeded him to the title. One of the latter's sons, Augustus, 3rd duke of Grafton, was prime minister for fifteen months between 1768 and 1770. The youngest son, George, created earl of Northumberland in 1674, married twice but left no issue by either wife.

Lady Anne Palmer (Fitzroy) married Thomas Lennard, 1st earl of Sussex and Baron Dacre. Their two sons died in infancy. The barony of Dacre became abeyant after Lennard's death in 1715, but the abeyance was terminated in 1741. The earldom was the fourth creation and likewise became abeyant, but there have subsequently been fifth, sixth, and seven creations. The sixth was another royal one, when Queen Victoria's third son, Arthur, became duke of Connaught and Strathearn, and earl of Sussex in 1874. It became abeyant on the death of his grandson, the 2nd duke (his son having predeceased him), in 1943, until the seventh creation. Charlotte Fitzroy (1664–1718) married Edward Lee, 1st earl of Lichfield. Their grandson, Robert, 4th earl of Lichfield, died childless in 1776 and the title became extinct until another creation at the coronation of King William IV in 1831. Of the two daughters who lived to maturity, the elder, Elizabeth, married twice, her second husband being the eighteenth-century poet Edward Young, and the younger, Barbara, married Sir George Browne, 3rd baronet of Kiddington.

Nell Gwyn's elder son, Charles Beauclerk, created duke of St Albans in 1684, and his wife, Lady Diana de Vere, daughter and heiress of the earl of Oxford, had nine sons and three daughters. The title duke of St Albans was passed down through the sons to the present day. Nell's younger son, James, died in infancy.

The only child of Louise de Kérouaille, duchess of Portsmouth in her own right, Charles Lennox, was created duke of Richmond in 1675. He married Anne Brudenell, and they had one son and two daughters. The title has likewise been passed down the generations from their son.

Mary 'Moll' Davis's daughter, Lady Mary Tudor, had three husbands. Her first was Edward Radcliffe, 2nd earl of Derwentwater, by whom she had three sons and one daughter. The second marriage to Henry Graham produced no children, but she had a daughter by the third, James Rooke. The male line of the family died out in 1814 with the passing of Anthony, 7th earl of Derwentwater, and with it the title.

APPENDIX II

LINES OF DESCENT TO MODERN ROYALTY

The blood of Charles II's children lives on in contemporary British royalty and will do so indefinitely. King Charles III can claim descent, not from any of them, but from King James VI and I through his granddaughter, Sophia, electress of Hanover. She was the mother of George, elector of Hanover and later King George I, first sovereign of the House of Hanover, from whom all subsequent monarchs are descended (had she lived another fifty-four days, Sophia would have succeeded Anne, her second cousin, as queen of Great Britain—at the age of eighty-three).

Both of King Charles III's wives can likewise not only trace their descent back to King James VI and I, but also, through different mistresses, to King Charles II. Lady Diana Spencer, whom he married in 1981, was the daughter of John, 8th Earl Spencer, who was a descendant of Henry Fitzroy, 1st duke of Grafton, son of Barbara, countess of Castlemaine, and at the same time of Charles Lennox, 1st duke of Richmond. As a result, William, prince of Wales, once he succeeds his father, will be the first king descended from 'The Merry Monarch'. Equally interesting is the descent of Earl Spencer and thus his children from King James II by one of his mistresses, Arabella Churchill. To stretch the family connections beyond royalty to politics, her brother, John, 1st duke of Marlborough, was an ancestor of twentieth-century Prime Minister Sir Winston Churchill.

Camilla Shand, now Queen Camilla, who King Charles III married in 2005 while he was still prince of Wales and heir to the throne, can trace her lineage through some of the earls of Albemarle and to Charles, 1st duke of Richmond and Lennox, the son of Louise de Kérouaille, duchess of Portsmouth.

Two more brides who married into the British royal family in the twentieth century can likewise count Charles II among their forebears. Alice, duchess of Gloucester, whose husband Duke Henry was the third son of King George V, was the daughter of John Montagu Douglas Scott, 7th duke of Buccleuch, and thus descended from the duke of Monmouth through his second son (and the eldest to reach maturity), James Scott, 1st earl of Dalkeith. Sarah, duchess of York, is similarly descended from the duke of Monmouth and earl of Dalkeith, her father, Ronald Ferguson, being the son of Marian Montagu Douglas Scott, granddaughter of William Henry Walter Montagu Douglas Scott, 6th duke of Buccleuch. In addition to this, she is also descended on her father's side from the duchess of Portsmouth's son, the duke of Richmond, and the countess of Castlemaine's eldest daughter, Anne, countess of Sussex.

APPENDIX III

THE CHILDREN OF CHARLES II

By **Lucy Barlow** (*c.* 1630–1658)

James Crofts, later Scott (1649–1685), created duke of Monmouth (1663) in England and duke of Buccleuch (1663) in Scotland; married Anne Scott, duchess of Buccleuch, 4 sons, 2 daughters; 1 son, 2 daughters by his mistress Eleanor Needham

Lucy Barlow's daughter, Mary Crofts (b. 1651) was not by Charles II

By **Elizabeth Killigrew** (1622–1680), married (1660) Francis Boyle, 1st Viscount Shannon

Charlotte Jemima Maria Fitzroy (1650–1684), married (1) James Howard, 1 daughter; (2) William Paston, 2nd earl of Yarmouth, 2 sons, 2 daughters (and others who died in infancy)

By **Catherine Pegge** (*c.* 1635–?)

Charles Fitzcharles (1657–1680), 'Don Carlos', created earl of Plymouth (1675), married Lady Bridget Osborne, no issue

Catherine Fitzcharles (1658-?), either died young or became a nun at Dunkirk

By **Barbara Villiers** (1640–1709), married (1659) Roger Palmer, 1st earl of Castlemaine, created duchess of Cleveland in her own right

Lady Anne Palmer (Fitzroy) (1661–1722), *sometimes thought to have been daughter of Roger Palmer, but King Charles, the more likely father, acknowledged her as his own;* married Thomas Lennard, 1st earl of Sussex and Baron Dacre, 2 sons, 2 daughters

Charles Fitzroy (1662–1730), created duke of Southampton (1675), became 2nd duke of Cleveland (1709), married (1) Mary Wood, (2) Anne Pulteney, 3 sons, 3 daughters

Henry Fitzroy (1663–90), created earl of Euston (1672), duke of Grafton (1675), married Isabella Bennet, 2nd countess of Arlington, 1 son

Charlotte Fitzroy (1664–1718), married Edward Lee, 1st earl of Lichfield, 13 sons, 5 daughters

George Fitzroy (1665–1716), created earl of Northumberland (1674), duke of Northumberland (1678), married (1) Catherine Wheatley, (2) Mary Dutton

Cecilia Fitzroy (1670/1–1759), probably daughter of Harry Jermyn, never acknowledged by King Charles

Barbara (Benedicta) Fitzroy (1672–1737), probably daughter of John Churchill, later duke of Marlborough, never acknowledged by King Charles

By **Nell (Eleanor) Gwyn** (1650–1687)

Charles Beauclerk (1670–1726), created duke of St Albans (1684), married Diana de Vere (1694), 9 sons, 2 daughters

James, Lord Beauclerk (1671–80)

By **Louise Renée de Penancoet de Kérouaille** (1649–1734), created duchess of Portsmouth in her own right (1673)

Charles Lennox (1672–1723), created duke of Richmond (1675) in England and duke of Lennox (1675) in Scotland; married Anne Brudenell, 1 son, 2 daughters

By **Mary 'Moll' Davis** (*c.* 1648–1708)

Lady Mary Tudor (1673–1726), married (1) Edward Radcliffe, 2nd earl of Derwentwater, 3 sons, 1 daughter; (2) Henry Graham; (3) James Rooke

ENDNOTES

Introduction

1. Longford, E., *Victoria R.I.* (London: Weidenfeld & Nicolson, 1964) p. 16.
2. Jesse, J. H., *Memoirs of the Court of England* (London: Henry Bohn, 1855), Vol. 3, p. 167.
3. Hough, R., *Louis & Victoria* (London: Hutchinson, 1974), p. 373.
4. Pepys, S., *Diary of Samuel Pepys* (London: Macmillan, 1905), 17 Aug. 1661, p. 96.

Chapter 1

1. Fraser, A., *King Charles II* (London: Weidenfeld & Nicolson, 1979), p. 10.
2. Hamilton, A., *Memoirs of Count Grammont* (London: Chatto & Windus, 1876), p. 190.
3. Pepys, *op. cit.*, 26 Apr. 1667, p. 488.
4. Clarendon, E., *History of the Rebellion and Civil Wars in England* (Oxford: Clarendon, 1888), Vol. 4, p. 23.
5. Wedgwood, C. V., *Trial of Charles I* (London: Collins, 1964), p. 130.
6. Evelyn, J., *Diary of John Evelyn* (London: Macmillan, 1906), 18 August 1649, Vol. I, p. 16.
7. Keay, A., *Last Royal Rebel* (London: Bloomsbury, 2016), p. 32.
8. Watson, J. N. P., *Captain-General and Rebel Chief* (London: Allen & Unwin, 1979), p. 8.
9. Scott, G., *Lucy Walter* (London: Harrap, 1947), p. 201.
10. Fraser, *op. cit.*, p. 64.
11. Porter, L., *Mistresses* (London: Picador, 2020), p. 160.
12. Cokayne, G., *Complete Peerage of England, Scotland, Ireland, etc.*, 2nd ed., 14 vols. (London: St Catherine Press, 1909–1959), Appendix F, p. 706.

Chapter 2

1. Steinman, G. Steinman, *Memoir of Barbara, Duchess of Cleveland* (Private circulation, 1871), p. 26.

2 Pepys, *op. cit.*, 26 Jul. 1662, p. 139.
3 Weir, A., *Britain's Royal Families* (London: Pimlico, 2002) p. 256.
4 Beauclerk-Dewar, P., & Powell, R., *Royal Bastards* (Stroud: History Press, 2008), p. 329.
5 Pepys, *op. cit.*, 26 Jul. 1665, p. 329.
6 Evelyn, *op. cit.*, 4 Nov. 1670, Vol. II, p.316; 1 Mar. 1671, Vol, 2, p. 321.
7 Del Mar, A., *Barbara Villiers* (New York: Cambridge Encyclopedia Co., 1899), p. 27.
8 Hamilton, E., *Illustrious Lady* (Hamish Hamilton, 1980), p. 69.
9 Pepys, 26 Apr. 1667, p. 489.
10 Sergeant, P. W., *My Lady Castlemaine* (London: Hutchinson, 1912), pp. 130-1.
11 Thompson, E., *Letters of Humphrey Prideaux to John Ellis, 1674–1722* (London: Camden Society, 1875), 17 Sept. 1674, p. 21.
12 *Ibid.*, 8 Nov. 1675, p. 48.
13 *Ibid.*, 31 Oct. 1676, pp. 55-6.
14 Andrews, A., *Royal Whore* (London: Hutchinson, 1971) p. 164n.
15 Thompson, *op. cit.*, 17 Sept. 1664, p. 58.
16 Sergeant, *op. cit.*, p. 111.
17 Pepys, *op. cit.*, 21 Feb. 1665, p. 303.
18 Jesse, *op. cit.*, Vol. 3, p. 171.
19 Jameson, A. *Beauties of the Court of Charles the Second* (London: Henry Bohn, 1833), p. 82.
20 *Archaeologia*, Charles II to Countess of Lichfield, 20 Oct. 1682, Vol. 57, Pt 1, p. 176.
21 Pepys, *op. cit.*, 30 Jul. 1667, p. 536.
22 Molloy, J., *Royalty Restored* (London: Ward & Downey, 1885), Vol. 2, p. 48.
23 Pepys, *op. cit.*, 7 Aug. 1667, p. 538.
24 *Ibid.*, 14 Jan. 1668, p. 604.
25 *Ibid.*, 31 May 1668, p. 656.
26 Evelyn, *op. cit.*, 1 Aug. 1672, Vol. 2, p. 350.
27 Pepys, *op. cit.*, 10 Sept. 1667, pp. 554-5.
28 Dasent, A., *Nell Gwyn* (London: Macmillan, 1924), p. 81.
29 Dasent A., *Private Life of Charles the Second* (London: Cassell, 1927), p. 170.
30 Beauclerk, pp. 220-1.
31 *Ibid.*, p. 280.
32 Evelyn, *op. cit.*, 9–10 Oct. 1671, Vol. 2, p. 331.
33 Williams, H., *Rival Sultanas* (London: Hutchinson, 1915), Croissy to Louvois, n.d., pp. 126-7.
34 Evelyn, *op. cit.*, 30 Mar. 1684, Vol. 3, p. 125.
35 Hutton, R., *Charles II* (Oxford: Clarendon Press, 1989, p. 279.
36 Bevan, B., *Charles II's French Mistress* (London: Robert Hale, 1972), *p. 79.*
37 *ODNB*, Wynne, *Eleanor [Nell] Gwyn.*
38 Forneron, H., *Court of Charles II, 1649–1734* (London: Swan Sonnenschein, 1886), Henri de Massué, Marquis de Ruvigny to Simon Arnauld, Marquis de Pomponne, 14 May 1674, p. 108.
39 Evelyn, *op. cit.*, 4 Oct. 1683, Vol. 3, p. 114.
40 Beauclerk-Dewar & Powell, *op. cit.*, p. 47.
41 *Ibid.*, p. 48.
42 Christie, W. (ed.), *Letters to Sir Joseph Williamson, 1673 and 1674,* 2 vols. (London: Camden Society, 1874), Vol. 2, T. Derham to J. Williamson, 5 Nov. 1673. pp. 62-3.
43 Evelyn, *op. cit.*, 6 Nov. 1679, Vol. 3, pp. 38-9.
44 Sergeant, *op. cit.*, p. 206.
45 Tweedie, Mrs A., *Hyde Park* (London: Eveleigh Nash, 1908), Grace, Viscountess Chaworth to Lord Ross, 25 Dec. 1676, p. 118.
46 Sergeant, *op. cit.*, p. 212.
47 Fraser, *op. cit.*, p. 343.
48 Andrews, *op. cit.*, p. 239.
49 Sergeant, *op. cit.*, p. 216.
50 Jesse, *op. cit.*, Countess of Castlemaine to King Charles II, 28 May 1678, Vol. 3, p. 170.

51 St Aubyn, G., *Queen Victoria* (London: Sinclair-Stevenson, 1991), p. 10.
52 Beauclerk, C., *Nell Gwyn* (London: Macmillan, 2005), p. 151.
53 Delpech, J., *Life & Times of the Duchess of Portsmouth* (London: Elek, 1953), p. 139.
54 Burnet, G., *History of my Own Time* (Oxford: Clarendon, 1897), Vol. 2, p. 432.
55 Turner, F. C., *James II* (Eyre & Spottiswoode, 1948), p. 164.
56 Beauclerk, *op. cit.*, p. 299.
57 Watson, *op. cit.*, p. 129.
58 Keay, *op. cit.*, pp. 296-7.
59 Fitzroy, Sir A., *Henry, Duke of Grafton* (Christophers, 1921), pp. 12-13.
60 *Ibid.*, earl of Arlington to duke of Ormond, 2 Oct. 1682, pp. 13-14.
61 Evelyn, *op. cit.*, 26 Oct. 1683, Vol. 3, p. 116.
62 *Ibid.*, 27 Oct. 1684, Vol. 3, p. 130.
63 Delpech, *op. cit.*, p. 170.
64 M'crie, T., ed., *Memoirs of Mr William Veitch, and George Brysson* (Edinburgh: Blackwood, 1825), pp. 158-9.
65 Welwood, J., *Memoirs of the Most Material Transactions in England* (London: Tim Goodwin, 1700), pp. 144-5.
66 Roberts, G., *Life, Progresses and Rebellion of James, Duke of Monmouth* (London: Longman, 1844), Vol 1. pp. 178-9.
67 Bryant, A., *King Charles II* (London: Longmans, Green, 1931), p. 389.
68 Watson, *op. cit.*, p. 188.
69 M'crie, T., *op. cit.*, p. 161.
70 *Ibid.*, p. 163.
71 Delpech, *op. cit.*, p. 182.
72 Fraser, *op. cit.*, p. 456.
73 Evelyn, *op. cit.*, 4 Feb. 1685, Vol. 3, pp. 140-2.
74 Burnet, *op. cit.*, Vol. 2, pp. 467-8.

Chapter 3

1 Evelyn, *op. cit.*, 4 Feb. 1685, Vol. 3, pp. 144-5.
2 M'crie, *op. cit.*, p. 165.
3 Keay, *op. cit.*, p. 332.
4 Seymour, W., *Battles in Britain* (London: Sidgwick & Jackson, 1975), pp. 172, 161.
5 Fitzroy, *op. cit.*, pp. 38-40.
6 Branston, p. 188.
7 Turner, *op. cit.*, p. 279.
8 Keay, *op. cit.*, pp. 372-3.
9 Seymour, W., *Sovereign Legacy* (London: Sidgwick & Jackson, 1979), p. 222.
10 Delpech, *op. cit.*, p. 185.
11 Sergeant, *op. cit.*, pp. 249-50.
12 Wilson, D., *All the King's Women* (London: Hutchinson, 2003), p. 152.
13 Fitzroy, *op. cit.*, p. 44.
14 Evelyn, *op. cit.*, 19 Feb. 1686, Vol. 3, p. 199.
15 *Ibid.*, 29 Mar. 1686, Vol. 3, p. 201.
16 Fitzroy, *op. cit.*, p. 47.
17 Jesse, *op. cit.*, Vol. 3, pp. 164-5.
18 *London Gazette*, n.d., Fitzroy, *op. cit.*, pp. 49-50.
19 Fitzroy, *op. cit.*, p. 52.
20 *Ibid.*, p. 54.
21 *Ibid.*, p. 59.
22 *Ibid.*, p. 64.

Chapter 4

1 Fitzroy, *op. cit.,* p. 65.
2 Macaulay, Lord, *Works* (London: Longmans, Green, 1871), Vol. 3, p. 330.
3 Fitzroy, *op. cit.,* p. 70.
4 *Ibid.*, p. 71.
5 Evelyn, *op. cit.,* 1 Aug. 1690, Vol. 3, p. 279.
6 Macaulay, *op. cit.,* Vol. 3, p. 331.
7 Finch, political papers, *ODNB*, Davies, *Henry, 1st Duke of Grafton.*
8 Jesse, *op. cit.,* Vol. 3, p. 163.
9 *Ibid.*, Vol. 3, p. 166.
10 *Foreign Post,* 7 Jul. 1697.
11 Forneron, *op. cit.,* p. 295.
12 March, Earl of, *Duke and his Friends* (Hutchinson, 1911), Vol. 1, p. 3.
13 Hearne, T., *Reliquiae Hearnianae* (London: John Russell Smith, 1869), 2 Jun. 1723, Vol. 2, p. 162.
14 Jesse, *op. cit.,* Vol. 3, p. 168.
15 March, *op. cit.,* duchess of Portsmouth to 2nd duke of Richmond, 26 Jun. 1723, translated from French, Vol. 1, p. 73.
16 Hervey, *Memoirs of the Reign of George the Second,* (John Murray, 1848), Vol. 1, pp. 251-2.
17 *Ibid.*, Vol. 3, p. 828.
18 Pearson, M., *Bright Tapestry* (Harrap, 1956), p. 22.

BIBLIOGRAPHY

All titles published in London unless stated otherwise

Andrews, A., *The Royal Whore: Barbara Villiers, Countess of Castlemaine* (Hutchinson, 1971)

Beauclerk, C., *Nell Gwyn: Mistress to a King* (Macmillan, 2005)

Beauclerk-Dewar, P., & Powell, R., *Royal Bastards: Illegitimate Children of the British Royal Family* (Stroud: History Press, 2008)

Bejiit, K. (ed.), *English Colonial Texts on Tangier, 1661–1684: Imperialism and the Politics of Resistance* (Abingdon: Routledge, 2015)

Bevan, B., *Charles II's French Mistress: A Biography of Louise de Kérouaille, Duchess of Portsmouth, 1649–1734* (Robert Hale, 1972); *James, Duke of Monmouth* (Robert Hale, 1973)

Branston, Sir J., *The Autobiography* (Camden Society, 1845)

Bryant, A., *King Charles II* (Longmans, Green, 1931)

Burnet, G., *History of my Own Time,* 3 vols. (Oxford: Clarendon, 1897)

Christie, W. (ed.), *Letters to Sir Joseph Williamson, 1673, 1674,* 2 vols. (Camden Society, 1874)

Clarendon, Edward, Earl of, *The History of the Rebellion and Civil Wars in England,* ed. W. Dunn, 6 vols. (Oxford: Clarendon, 1888)

Cokayne, G., *The Complete Peerage of England, Scotland, Ireland, Great Britain and the United Kingdom,* 2nd ed., 14 vols. (St Catherine Press, 1909–1959)

Dasent, A., *Nell Gwyn, 1650–1687: Her life story from St Giles's to St James's* (Macmillan, 1924); *The Private Life of Charles the Second* (Cassell, 1927)

Delpech, J., *The Life & Times of the Duchess of Portsmouth* (Elek, 1953)

Del Mar, A., *Barbara Villiers: Or, A History of Monetary Crimes* (New York: Cambridge Encyclopedia Co., 1899)

Evelyn, J., *The Diary of John Evelyn,* 3 vols. (Macmillan, 1906)

Fitzroy, Sir A., *Henry, Duke of Grafton, 1663–1690* (Christophers, 1921)

Forneron, H., *The Court of Charles II, 1649–1734* (Swan Sonnenschein, 1886)

Fraser, A., *King Charles II* (Weidenfeld & Nicolson, 1979)

Hamilton, A., *Memoirs of Count Grammont* (Chatto & Windus, 1876)

Hamilton, E., *The Illustrious Lady: A Biography of Barbara Villiers, Countess of Castlemaine and Duchess of Cleveland* (Hamish Hamilton, 1980)

Hearne, T., *Reliquiae Hearnianae: The Remains of Thomas Hearne,* 3 vols. (John Russell Smith, 1869)

Hervey, Lord, *Memoirs of the Reign of George the Second,* 2 vols. (John Murray, 1848)

Hilliam, D., *Kings, Queens, Bones and Bastards: Who's Who in the English Monarchy from Egbert to Elizabeth II* (Stroud: Sutton, 1998)
Hough, R., *Louis & Victoria: The First Mountbattens* (Hutchinson, 1974)
Hutton, R., *Charles II, King of England, Scotland and Ireland* (Oxford: Clarendon Press, 1989)
Jameson, A. *The Beauties of the Court of Charles the Second: A Series of Memoirs Biographical and Critical* (Henry Bohn, 1833)
Jesse, J. H., *Memoirs of the Court of England during the Reign of the Stuarts*, 3 vols. (Henry Bohn, 1855)
Keay, A., *The Last Royal Rebel: The Life and Death of James, Duke of Monmouth* (Bloomsbury, 2016)
Longford, E., *Victoria R.I.* (Weidenfeld & Nicolson, 1964)
Macaulay, Lord, *The Works of Lord Macaulay*, 8 vols, ed. H. Macaulay (Longmans, Green, 1871)
March, Earl of (Charles Gordon-Lennox, 8th Duke of Richmond), *A Duke and his Friends: The Life and Letters of the Second Duke of Richmond*, 2 vols. (Hutchinson, 1911)
M'crie, T., ed., *Memoirs of Mr William Veitch, and George Brysson* (Edinburgh: Blackwood, 1825)
Molloy, J., *Royalty Restored or London under Charles II*, 2 vols. (Ward & Downey, 1885)
Pearson, M., *Bright Tapestry* (Harrap, 1956)
Pepys, S., *The Diary of Samuel Pepys* (Macmillan, 1905)
Porter, L., *Mistresses: Sex and Scandal at the Court of Charles II* (Picador, 2020)
Pritchard, R., *Scandalous Liaisons: Charles II and his Court* (Amberley, 2015)
Roberts, G., *The Life, Progresses and Rebellion of James, Duke of Monmouth*, 2 vols. (Longman, Brown, Green and Longman, 1844)
Scott, G., *Lucy Walter, Wife or Mistress* (Harrap, 1947)
Sergeant, P. W., *My Lady Castlemaine: Being a Life of Barbara Villiers, Countess of Castlemaine, afterwards Duchess of Cleveland* (Hutchinson, 1912)
Seymour, W., *Battles in Britain: And their Political Background* (Sidgwick & Jackson, 1975); *Sovereign Legacy: An Historical Guide to the British Monarchy* (Sidgwick & Jackson, 1979)
Simms, J. G., *War and Politics in Ireland, 1649–1730* (A. & C. Black, 1986)
Steinman, G. Steinman, *A Memoir of Barbara, Duchess of Cleveland* (Printed for private circulation, 1871)
St Aubyn, G., *Queen Victoria: A Portrait* (Sinclair-Stevenson, 1991)
Thompson, E., *Letters of Humphrey Prideaux to John Ellis, 1674–1722* (Camden Society, 1875)
Turner, F. C., *James II* (Eyre & Spottiswoode, 1948)
Tweedie, Mrs A., *Hyde Park, Its History and Romance* (Eveleigh Nash, 1908)
Waller, M., *Ungrateful Daughters: The Stuart Princesses who Stole their Father's Crown* (Hodder & Stoughton, 2002)
Watson, J. N. P., *Captain-General and Rebel Chief: The Life of James, Duke of Monmouth* (Allen & Unwin, 1979)
Wedgwood, C. V., *The Trial of Charles I* (Collins, 1964)
Weir, A., *Britain's Royal Families: The Complete Genealogy* (Pimlico, 2002)
Welwood, J., *Memoirs of the Most Material Transactions in England, for the Last Hundred Years preceding the Revolution in 1688* (Tim Goodwin, 1700)
Williams, H., *Rival Sultanas: Nell Gwyn, Louise de Kéroualle, and Hortense Mancini* (Hutchinson, 1915)
Wilson, D., *All the King's Women: Love, Sex and Politics in the Life of Charles II* (Hutchinson, 2003)
Wilson, J., *Court Satires of the Restoration* (Ohio: State University Press, 1976)
Zee, H. & B., *William and Mary* (Macmillan, 1973)

Archeologia
Oxford Dictionary of National Biography

INDEX